Industrywide
Voluntary
Product Standards

Industrywide Voluntary Product Standards

David Hemenway

Ballinger Publishing Company ● Cambridge, Mass.
A Subsidiary of J.B. Lippincott Company

10256 9

International Standard Book Number: 0–88410–275–0

Library of Congress Catalog Card Number: 74–28269

Printed in the United States of America

Library of Congress Cataloging in Publication Data

Hemenway, David.
  Industrywide voluntary product standards
  Bibliography: p.
  1. Standardization—United States. I. Title.
T59.2.U6H45   389.6'0973   74–28269
ISBN 0–88410–275–0

Table of Contents

Acknowledgments

Acknowledgments

I am indebted to many people in government, trade associations, and engineering societies who granted me interviews and answered my detailed letters. I am especially grateful to a hero, Ralph Nader, who aroused my interest in this subject.

In academia, I would like to thank Richard E. Caves for his careful reading and helpful comments concerning the manuscript; A. Michael Spence for his encouragement and insights; and most of all my advisor Thomas C. Schelling, who long ago convinced me that economics need not be dull.

Part I

Introduction

Chapter One

Introduction

In February 1904 a great blaze broke out in downtown Baltimore. So serious did the fire become that help was solicited from surrounding communities. Washington, D.C., fire engines reached the scene within three hours, and additional units later arrived from as far afield as Annapolis, Wilmington, Chester, York, Altoona, Harrisburg, Philadelphia, and New York. Unfortunately, most of these units proved of little assistance, for their hoses would not fit Baltimore hydrants. Though there was never a shortage of water many fire fighting units had to stand by, virtually helpless, as the fire raged for over thirty hours, destroying more than 1,500 buildings and all the electric light, telephone, telegraph, and power facilities in an area of seventy city blocks.[1]

The need for uniform screw threads had long been recognized in most advanced industrial societies. In England, the screw thread standard proposed in 1841 by Sir Joseph Whitworth in an historic communication to the Institution of Civil Engineers soon won acceptance and became known as the British Standard Whitworth thread. In the United States, a major attempt to create a standard American screw thread was made by one William Sellers. In an 1864 paper read before Franklin Institute, he argued: "In this country no organized attempt has as yet been made to establish any system (of screw threads), each manufacturer having adopted whatever his judgment may have dictated as the best, or as most convenient for himself, but ... so radical a defect should be allowed to exist no longer."[2] The standard proposed by Sellers was gradually adopted in North America. That the system did not immediately and completely pervade the American economy is illustrated by the Baltimore tragedy and by the fact that as late as 1964 fire fighters in a county contiguous to Baltimore were still being confronted with two types of hydrants in use, one with the national thread standard, and the other with the Baltimore steamer thread.[3]

3

In other countries, similar catastrophes have occurred due to the absence of a fully implemented material screw thread standard. In the thirties, for example, the south German city of Oeschelbronn burned to the ground while neighboring fire brigades stood by helplessly. Today West Germany has not only standardized its hoses and hydrants, but has developed one of the world's most comprehensive systems of standards and specifications.[4]

Even with the adoption of a standard screw thread in North America, major difficulties continued internationally due to differences between the Seller and Whitworth (and other) systems. Though the differences between the two systems were slight—sides of grooves sloping at 60° instead of 55°, and bottoms of grooves being flat with sharp corners instead of rounded—they were enough to prevent the interchange of the two systems of threads. During the Second World War, for example, many damaged American tanks in North Africa remained immobilized simply because British fasteners could not be used for repair purposes.[5] It would wait until 1948 before a uniform screw thread agreement was signed by the United States, Canada, and Britain. There is now an International Screw Thread Standard, though it is not universally followed.[6]

The screw thread standards of the nineteenth century were perhaps the first modern industrial or engineering standards established for public, as distinct from private, use. (Earlier private engineering standards would include Eli Whitney's production of interchangeable gun parts, or the Brund-Maudslay mass-production of standardized pulley blocks.)[7] Formal industrywide or national standardization of products did not really begin in the United States until near the turn of the twentieth century. Some early examples of successful standardization were the 1921 reduction in the variety of paving brick from sixty-six different sizes to eleven, the rigid definitions of "manganese steel" and "nickel steel," and the 1914 Boiler Code for safety. Such industrywide voluntary product standards form the focal point for the present paper.

FUNDAMENTAL STANDARDS

Standards can be broadly defined as something taken for a basis of comparison, or that which is accepted for current use through authority, custom or general consent. In a sense, then, standards, are at least as old as man. Fashions of dress or social mores could be considered standards. Reading from top to bottom on a page, and driving on the right are conventions or standards. On a different level, one might argue that natural selection breeds standardization. The Socratic "forms" would be obvious standards.

Before proceeding to the main topic of this book, it is useful to consider four fundamental types of standards. They concern time, numbers, language, and other "weights and measures." Before the vast improvements in transportation and communication in the late nineteenth century there was little need for standard time zones. Local communities usually had their own time.

Noon in Boston might be 11:56 in Worcester, noon in Chicago 12:06 in Indianapolis. It was the coming of the railroads and the telegraph that shrank the world enough to eventually force national (and international) standardization. The railroad companies themselves were among the principal actors in the creation of our standard time zones. Initially each company had adopted its own official time, but much confusion and delay resulted when transfers were necessary, and it was important to make the right connections. Such complications need not have arisen, of course, had there been a monopoly railway. The various companies, however, soon agreed together on a standard plan, marking off convenient time-zones with hourly changes at each boundary. The essence of the railroad agreement became our official zones in 1918 when Congress commissioned, indicatively, the Interstate Commerce Commission to draw the boundaries. What is occasionally referred to as "God's Time" is only a recent man-made standard, originally pushed by the railroads and "administered" by the ICC.[8]

The calendar is merely an agreed upon standard or convention. So is what year it is, when the year begins, or when the day begins. The Year of our Lord 1973, for example, is 5734 in the Jewish calendar. Rosh Hashanah celebrates the Jewish new year (about the time of the autumnal equinox), rather than at January first. In our colonial days, March 25 (mistakenly thought to be the vernal equinox) marked the New Year. Ending the day at midnight is another convention. Astronomers as late as 1924 ended the day at noon so as not to break up nightly observation. Throughout history, sunrise or sunset has often been considered as the beginning, or end, of the day. At one time daytime and nightime were defined as both consisting of twelve hours. As days lengthened over the year, so did the length of a daytime hour. The "eleventh hour" was always the last one before sunset.[9]

The length of the day is another standard. It is defined as the time it takes the earth to make a complete revolution, with respect to the sun, from the viewpoint of an observer on the earth. A man on the moon, however, sees the earth making such a revolution in a little over twenty-three of our current hours—the lunar day. While such a frame of reference is equally as valid, it is not nearly as useful (though it would make the timing of the tides appear more uniform), nor easily comprehensible. It has never been in contention as "the real" day.

Roman numerals are equally as valid as arabic, but the latter are clearly more practicable, and rapidly gained sway upon reaching Europe in the High Middle Ages. Presently arabic numerals are used almost universally, which in itself greatly facilitates communication. Written language, however, has never reached such levels of international standardization. The English language itself is not completely standardized—there is, for example, no official dictionary— and is probably far from optimal. The grammar is overly complex, the spelling troublesome (e.g. rough, through, though, cough, hiccough). Even the widely accepted Roman alphabet has real drawbacks. There is, for example, evidence that a simplified alphabet can help children read English, an alphabet without capital letters but with such sounds added as ae, au, ie, sh, ou, ie.[10]

What benefits and costs could be expected from international standardization of language? Broadly speaking ones similar in nature to those arising from most examples of simplification or reduction in varieties. Usually communication is facilitated, and costs reduced (in this case, the cost of learning other languages, translating, interpreting, etc.). The costs could include any changeover costs (large in this case), plus the reduction of possibly desired diversity and variety. The question of international language standardization under current circumstances is perhaps academic, for people would have to agree not only on the desirability of a universal language, but also on what that language should be.

On the other hand, the goal of a universal weights and measures system has nearly been achieved. The metric system, a gift from the French Reign of Terror, was *consciously designed* (unlike our languages). It is simple and convenient, and generally acknowledged as a superior to the Customary system (which has itself been simplified from the days of fothers of lead and punches of prunes, firkins and kilderkins, coons, strikes, and pottles).[11]

While the United States remains one of the last strongholds of the Customary system, we are *officially* a metric nation! The United States received standard meter bars and kilogram weights in 1884, and four years later the Secretary of the Treasury, by administrative order, declared these to be the nation's "fundamental standards" of length and mass. We have never had a legal material standard yard or pound. These and other customary units are defined as functions of the standard metric units.[12] This book will not enter into the long running controversy of whether the United States should really "go metric." Suffice it to say that the costs are primarily the changeover or conversion costs, the benefits are those to be derived from going on a more universal system, plus going on a better (easier to teach, etc.) system.

There are clear benefits that arise from a uniform (and convenient) national system of weights and measures. Governments have long recognized that the lack of such uniform standards not only hinder trade and commerce, but could also impede the collection of taxes. Henry I of England in 1120 decreed that henceforth the "ell" would be the exact length of his arm, and that this exact distance should be the standard unit of comparison throughout his kingdom.[13] Easier said than done, of course. The framers of our Constitution reserved many powers for the states, but understood the need for uniform national standards and thus gave Congress the sole authority to fix weights and measures. Authority is not enough. Even in this century, in Brooklyn, at one time four different "feet" were being accepted concurrently, the U.S. foot, the Bushwick foot, the Williamsburg foot, and the foot of the 26th ward.[14]

The creation of officially sanctioned weights and measures is clearly not sufficient to achieve actual uniformity. The problem is not only one of over-coming local standards, but of preventing commercial debasement of the official one. "Chiseling" derived from actual chiseling down of standard weights and measures), giving short weight, and like deceptive practices are of ancient origin. Throughout the Bible, for example, there are injunctions such as that of Proverbs 11.1: "A false balance is abomination to the Lord, but a just weight is his delight." The attempt to chisel normally makes sense because the chiseler believes that information is incomplete. (With complete information about the product, but not about demand and supply curves, attempts to chisel might be considered as bargaining tactics.) True deception or fraud presumes the exis-tence of an asymmetry of knowledge between the buyer and the seller.

An incentive to debase weight and measure standards in actual commercial practice, and difficulties in discovering debasement, has meant that some enforcement of these standards has been necessary to maintain their useful-ness. The incentive to cheat, combined with the difficulty of detection, has not been so prevalent, and there has been less need to enforce the standards previously described—time zones, calendars, numbers, and language. Such standards are often used in more purely cooperative than competitive situations. If the ICC, as an example, draws reasonable time boundaries, it need not spend much time enforcing them. Language is really a convention, has not been formally standardized, and change is easy, permissible, and expected. Com-mercial contract language, of course, needs to be enforced, and is done so by the courts. There could be a strong incentive to debase the standard hour (actually a "weights and measure") to work 58 minutes for an hours pay. But detection is easy, and most such attempts are doomed to failure.

One last word on these standards. The very existence of generally accepted standards and conventions creates something of a dichotomy. You either follow the standard, or you don't. And there are some incentives not to, a principal one being to distinguish yourself. Street or ghetto talk, for example, could be considered such an attempt (and also to flout the convention, improve the language, etc.) as can a doctor's jargon.[15] One way Nepal may indicate her independence from neighboring India is by ignoring the conventional one hour time zones and staying ten minutes ahead of Indian Standard Time.[16]

INDUSTRYWIDE VOLUNTARY
PRODUCT STANDARDS

The focus of the present book is on more specific standards than those general "standards" of language, numbers, time, and weights and measures, which under-lie all other standards. The topic is collective or industrywide voluntary product standards. The emphasis is thus upon standards for public use rather than a company's internal quality control procedures. The discussion principally con-cerns voluntary rather than mandatory standards, and products rather than services. Accreditation, certification, and licensing will be mentioned only to further illuminate the role of product standards in the American economy.

Ironically, standards have not been completely standardized. There is not, for example, exact agreement on the definition of a standard. No format has been widely adopted for the writing of formal standards. Types of standards often mentioned in the literature include: standards of terminology or definition, standards of dimension, of safety, of quality, of identity; standards of practice, of test procedures, of information disclosure; standard specifications.

This book distinguishes between two principal types of product standards—standards of quality, and standards for uniformity (often dimensional standards) where "better" or "worse" is not the issue, but sameness or uniformity is. Screw thread standards, for example, are basically dimensional standards. It usually matters little for the performance of a screw whether the grooves are at a 55°, 60°, or 50° angle. As we have seen however, it may be extremely important that the angle be the same for all screws.

Another example of an early and important standard for uniformity is the railroad track gauge standard. It makes little difference whether the standard distance between tracks is 7 feet, as on the original Great Western Railroad, 5'6" as in South America, or 3'6" as in South Africa. It does matter, however, whether there is a uniform national standard. Following England's lead, the United States chose 4'8½" as its standard gauge, and most of our railroads had switched to this gauge by the time of the Civil War. Combined with a system of interchangeable brakes and coupling this made possible the interchangeability of rolling stock among virtually all roads throughout the nation. Australia, on the other hand, through most of the twentieth century never adopted a uniform standard. Thus when cargoes are transferred there is usually the inconvenience and cost of reloading, or special undertrucks are required.[17]

Other examples of standards for uniformity are those for record sizes and record player speeds (33-1/3, 45, 78 rpm), bed sizes (king, queen, double, twin), and electric lamp sockets, (which are mainly of one type in the United States, the Edison base). Standards for uniformity mean the deliberate reduction of variety, sometimes to one type (as railroad gauges), sometimes to a number (as bed sizes). Deliberate reduction of product variety in an entire market is often identified with the term simplification. This book distinguishes between those cases where the fundamental purpose of simplification is increased interchangeability, and those cases where it is not. Such a division is not clear-cut, and there are many standards for uniformity where classification would be difficult and arbitrary. Certainly, though, most of the standards discussed thus far belong in the former category. They exist primarily for the interchangeability of various manufacturers records and phonographs, beds and sheets, bulbs and lamps. While all simplification permits some interchangeability, broadly defined, (e.g. standard traffic lights,) for some standards, the more important effects concern economies of scale or market information rather than interchangeability. Examples of such standards include the simplification of tacks, files, and beer can sizes.

Quality standards are a second major type of standard, distinguished in this book from standards for uniformity. Such standards are universally minimum rather than maximum standards. They divide products into categories of better (meeting the standard) and worse (not meeting the standard), superior and inferior. Quality standards are more likely to require "enforcement" than are standards for uniformity. Sellers generally have a great incentive to cheat, to pass off inferior products as superior. And buyers usually have more difficulty in judging quality than, say, some dimensional uniformity needed for interchangeability. Compared to such simple quality characteristics as tensile strength or caloric content, physical dimensions generally are more readily apparent, easily and acceptably measurable, and dimensional interchangeability quickly determinable.

Some examples of standards classified here as quality standards include standards of identity (as the mandatory USDA standards that "peanut butter" must contain at least 90 per cent peanuts by weight, that "orange drink" must consist of at least 10 per cent orange juice), safety standards (as industrywide voluntary standards for such products as power tools or step-ladders), as well as those standards more conventionally characterized as quality or performance standards (as the cement and concrete standards which specify not only the proportions of constituent materials, but also provide strict guidelines controlling the mixing, transporting, placing, and curing of the concrete). Also, in order to encompass most important standards, those for measurement and testing are considered under the rubric of quality standards.

The distinction between standards for uniformity and quality standards seems important, but is sometimes blurred in the real world. Many quality standards, for example, allow interchangeability, permitting users to confidently substitute one manufacturers part for anothers. On the other hand, while dimensional characteristics are often most important for interchangeability, the function of some dimensional standards appears to be principally to assure minimum quality levels. Thus yard lumber size standards (as that standard of identity defining the 2 by 4 board as 1½″ by 3½″) are probably fundamentally quality standards to prevent adulteration, and are discussed as such in this book.

NEGLECTED, BUT IMPORTANT TOPIC

Voluntary standardization has received scant attention from economists. Economists, for example, rarely testify at the relevant congressional hearings. Modern Industrial Organization tests often ignore the entire topic. In fact, there has been virtually nothing specifically about standardization in economic periodicals for the last twenty years.

In 1961 economist R. Brady argued, with little success, for increased interest in this broad topic:

> It would be difficult to cite a single instance in the whole history of the rise of modern industrial methods where the need for complete, exhaustive and painstaking reexamination is more badly needed than here [standardization] ... Economists are almost unaware of its problems. Ultimate consumers scarcely know the meaning of the word.[18]

The academic interest of other professionals has generally kept pace with that of the economist's. In 1969, for example, lawyer Marian Opala, could, with some justification, write:

> Neither the nature of the non-governmental standards-making process nor its impact on the laws has received much attention, if any, in the legal literature of recent years.[19]

Yet industrywide voluntary product standards can and do have a significant effect on the economy and on society. A collective industrywide decision, for example, concerning what product characteristics are important and what quality levels constitute above or below standard can have a tremendous impact on competition and competitors, on industry structure, conduct, and performance. The simple selection of the appropriate measuring rod and test methods can be crucial, just as the decisions on how we measure "Gross National Product" or "Inflation," "Unemployment," and "Poverty" profoundly influence public policy choices.

The fact that many voluntary product standards become mandatory local, state, and federal standards underlines their importance. The National Electric Code, for example, despite minor modifications at the local level, provides 95 per cent of the electrical safety regulations in use in the United States.[20] The American Society of Mechanical Engineers (ASME) Boiler and Pressure Vessel Code has been adopted by most states and by Canada.[21] The Society of Automotive Engineers (SAE) technical standards are widely used by both the Federal Aviation Administration[22] and National Highway Safety Bureau[23] as a basis for establishing standards. Administrators of the new Occupational Health and Safety Act are required to look first to existing voluntary standards, and over 120 such standards have already been adopted.[24] And in exonerating the American Society for Testing and Materials (ASTM) in an asbestos-cement price fixing case, the District Court of Pennsylvania went so far as to say:

> Because of the heavy reliance of federal, state and municipal governments upon ASTM for specifications, the Society may be

regarded as an essential arm, or branch, of the government, and its acts may be entitled to the immunity from antitrust laws accorded governmental acts.[25]

The United States voluntary standardization system is important, and does deserve some attention from social scientists. It is the broad purpose of this book to generally describe and discuss voluntary product standards in the United States—for the first time from the viewpoint of an economist. This book is far from a comprehensive study of the system. Its basic aim is to give the reader a "feel" for the role of voluntary standards, and some further insights into the workings of our economy.

In order to prevent the discussion from getting out of hand it is important to limit the topic somewhat. This book is about industrywide voluntary product standards. The focus is *not* on internal company standards, nor mandatory standards, nor service standards. Other areas of interest *not* the principal concern of this book include historical standardization (as guilds) or the history of U.S. standards; international standardization, or standard setting in other developed countries, the potential for the less developed, or the metric system controversy. Nor are the antitrust implications, nor the certification and enforcement problems of standards a primary focus here.

It does, however, seem necessary to keep the topic fairly broad since the entire subject has so rarely been examined. Unfortunately standardization is intimately involved with a number of important areas economists have somewhat neglected—e.g., quality as an economic variable, and the economics of information. Other such issues involve interindustry competition, nonprofit organizations, and collective action. All of these areas, to some degree or another, must be discussed in this book. The topic thus becomes very broad.

Thus, to be manageable, the discussion must be quite selective, and one line of analysis is generally followed. First the benefits and costs of various standards are discussed. Then the incentive and ability to create workable standards are analyzed, specifically in their relation to certain market structure characteristics. Finally, there emerge a few recommendations for public policy.

Chapter 2 analyzes in depth a particular case study, and uses this to illustrate a number of crucial aspects of standards-creation. The focus is on the underlying forces that cause (or prevent) such industrywide standardization. The economics of tying proves helpful when considering interchangeability standards.

Chapters 3 through 5 deal with quality standards. The important discussion of the economies of information is reserved until Chapter 6. Chapter 7 examines in depth the incentives of buyers and sellers to create minimum standards. Chapter 8 contains a description of the current United States voluntary standards system. In the ninth and final chapter is a summary and conclusions.

Early American Automobile Standards: A Case Study

Given the general lack of information about standards, it seems appropriate at this juncture to present an in-depth case study. One has appeared in the economic literature, and it nicely illustrates a number of important points. The case history deals with the beginnings of industrywide standardization in the early American automobile industry.

The automobile industry was one of the first to achieve marked success in intercompany technical standardization. It was well recognized, as early as 1900, that industrywide standardization could bring substantial benefits to this industry. Automobile manufacturing was composed of a large number of small firms with a growing dependence on one another for parts, materials, and services. The time was ripe for intercompany standardization to facilitate procurement, exchange, servicing, and repair.[1]

The simple realization of the advantages to be gained through intercompany standards, however, did not automatically produce an effective program. In the decade following 1900 there were sporadic attempts to establish standards for wheel rims, spark plugs, screw threads, and even for steel specifications, but these met with little success. It was not until 1910 that two new factors combined together to create a viable standards system. The first of these factors was the brief, but severe, economic crisis that gripped the new industry, accentuating the need for standards. The second was the recent establishment of a body of professional automotive engineers, without trade association entanglements, that was eminently capable of creating acceptable technical standards.[2]

One could expect instability and periodic crises in the infant automobile industry, an industry composed of many small firms selling a new, experimental, expensive, and highly durable consumer product. The small automobile firms were primarily assemblers. They had difficulty in attracting large sums of capital, and generally economized on capital by purchasing most of their parts from outside, instead of building their own plant facilities. While this helped alleviate their financial problems, it often forced them to tie their own well-being to the fate of a few specific supplier companies.[3]

The small automobile concern was initially exposed to the competition of large-scale enterprise in the first decade of this century. In 1908 the General Motors combine was formed, and by 1910 had gathered in some twenty smaller companies controlling 20 per cent of the market. The Ford Model T was in production in 1908, and within two years accounted for 10 per cent of industry sales. The automobile manufacturers trade association collapsed in 1910, a year of economic crisis for small assemblers. Eighteen auto companies failed that year (a sharp rise from the average of one per year in the preceding seven years), along with numerous suppliers of parts. Many of the remaining producers faced similar ruin, partly due to their dependence on specific suppliers.[4]

In 1910 parts were manufactured according to the peculiar specifications of each company. Should a supplier go out of business—a supplier of even such minor items as bolts, washers, or tubing—his customers, specific automobile assemblers, could find themselves in dire straits. This was especially true for the smaller automobile firms who could not economically distribute orders for single parts among several suppliers. Before additional parts of the same specification could be secured, another supplier might have to make tool and jigs, or possibly build entirely new machinery for their production. During the interim, assembly operations might be ground to a standstill.[5]

While delivery delays could at any time interfere with assembly operations, it was in 1910 that general problems became sufficiently severe to lead to earnest and renewed attempts at standardization. The new Society of Automobile Engineers was the logical and appropriate place for such activities. SAE members possessed the technical expertise needed for standardization, represented both suppliers and purchasers, and most important, were themselves personally threatened by the industry crisis. Furthermore, the president of the SAE, Howard Coffin, vigorously promoted standards, claiming the lack of intercompany standards were "responsible for nine-tenths of the production troubles and most of the needless expense entailed in the manufacture of motor cars."[6]

By 1921 the SAE had created and published 224 different sets of standards. Many were widely used. A 1915 questionnaire, for example, found 94 per cent of companies responding using SAE screw and bolt standards, 90 per cent the lock washer and wheel and rim standards, and 93 per cent the spark plug standard. There were numerous generous estimates of the benefits of standardization. In 1916 the National Automobile Chamber of Commerce, an industry trade association, called the SAE program "one of the greatest factors in the upbuilding of the industry as it is today." They estimated that SAE cost savings led to a 30 per cent reduction in the cost of ball bearings and electrical equipment, and a 20 per cent reduction in steel costs. A writer for the industry trade journal claimed that standards accounted for annual savings of $750 million, or 15 per cent of the retail value of automobiles.[7]

The early SAE standards dealt primarily with dimensions of parts and accessories, and were designed to reduce variety and promote interchangeability. Thus steel tubing varieties were reduced from 1,100 to 150, lock washers from 300 designs to 35. Wheels and rims, generator mountings and carburetor flanges, spark plugs and screw threads were all standardized to promote interchangeability.[8]

These parts standards were principally of value to the smaller concerns. They made the automobile manufacturer less dependent on particular suppliers, and the suppliers less dependent on specific buyers. Use of intercompany standards also permitted longer runs and economies of scale in parts production even though individual orders remained small. For the automobile assemblers this meant better deliveries, lower prices, and probably higher quality. These were the types of benefits the large-scale automobile producer could achieve via internal standardization and large orders. Furthermore, the major firms were beginning to manufacture most of their own parts.[9]

The early standards committees were, indeed, dominated by representatives of the smaller companies. As the industry matured, however, and the small firms—despite the benefits from SAE standards—gradually gave way before the large-scale enterprises, the character and direction of the standards program also shifted. As engineers from the giant concerns (except Ford) came to control the committees the emphasis of the program changed from detailed parts standards (as those for differentials, door hinges, steering wheel hubs, generator brushes, etc.) to standards that were also of prime value to the large-scale enterprise. For example, in the 20s and 30s more standard interindustry purchase specifications were written (as steel specifications, as contrasted with those for auto parts), along with standards promoting efficient automobile operation (as SAE oil standards).[10]

Even in the early years of the SAE, General Motors played an important role in promoting steel specifications, while displaying little interest for detailed parts standards. The establishment of standards for alloy steel may well be the most important single accomplishment of the SAE, yet it was here that the standards program met its bitterest opposition. While some wheel manufacturers had fought standards (especially, one suspects, those whose products did not match the dimensional standard), and some oil refineries opposed the SAE standard viscosity ratings in the 20s, nowhere was the struggle against standards so intense as in the steel industry.[11]

The rule of the 1910 steel salesman seems to have been "special brands, secret processes and mysterious ingredients"[12] —combined with high prices and delays in delivery. Established steel manufacturers were understandably reluctant to relinquish brand advantages, and thus saw little direct benefit from providing detailed product information to buyers and helping them coordinate their purchases. The general attitude of the steel industry was perhaps typified by the sarcastic comment of a steel spring executive: "I say it is none of your business, Mr. Coffin, if I make my springs of pot metal. What is it to you, if they carry a car and never break."[13]

But SAE standard specifications were written for steel, and generally supported by the automobile manufacturers, who were able to impose them on suppliers. Standard specifications were soon widely used by automobile companies when purchasing from the steel, rubber, petroleum, and machine product industries. (Standards are not appropriable and are thus also available to any firm buying from those industries.) The collection of SAE standards–the SAE handbook–quickly became the "bible" of the automotive engineer.[14]

The story of the early SAE provides examples of both uniformity and quality standards, and illustrates a great many important aspects of industrywide standardization. Three general topics deserve immediate comment: (1) The possible benefits to society of industry-wide standards; (2) The fact that there is no automatic mechanism insuring that such beneficial standards will be produced; (3) The role of buyers with power in promoting intercompany standards.

1. In many situations, the self-interested actions of individual decisionmakers may lead to less than optimal outcomes. Moving away from the strict assumptions of perfect competition, for example, allowing information problems and externalities, we may find that collective action can increase social welfare. Track gauge standards, for example, may not emerge without intercompany cooperation, yet may be highly beneficial. This was true, historically, of screw thread standards, early auto part uniformities, standard steel specifications, the Boiler Code, etc. This book spends a great deal of time discussing those situations when intercompany standards may prove useful, and when they are not likely to emerge. The point here is simply that they provide one possible method, generally by *collective* action, of increasing welfare in the real world.

2. The fact that standardization generally requires conscious collective action may mean that there is no automatic *market* mechanism to insure the creation of beneficial standards. Thus automatic parts standards which in 1900 might have benefited all directly concerned–automobile assemblers, their suppliers, and the ultimate consumer–had to wait for a severe crisis and the emergence of an organization capable of writing acceptable standards. There might have been shortrun change-over problems for specific firms, but the delay was probably due to lack of familiarity with standardization and each other, problems of communication, trust, or understanding, or plain inertia. The point to be made is that the difficulties of many independent, autonomous decisionmakers in agreeing on a course of action–even one beneficial to all–is an order above, say, those internal problems a firm has in trying to make rational

choices. Moreover, the "discipline of the market" is absent, *if* those progressive firms pushing for standards are hurt as much or more by the lack of standards than are those "inefficient" firms who successfully opposed them.

And the fact that standards generally provide collective benefits may pose problems. If standards are what Mancur Olsen, Jr. calls "inclusive collective goods,"[15] benefiting all firms whether or not they helped create the standard (e.g., anyone may use an SAE standard), there may be little incentive for a rational, self-interested firm to participate in the (somewhat) costly writing process. The problem is one of positive externalities, similar to the "free rider" issue for unions. For groups composed of many small participants--with no coercion or outside inducements or selective incentives--there might be an inadequate provision of standards. This might be one reason why present standardization activities are dominated by large-scale enterprises who internalize more of the benefits. It may explain the slight air of self-sacrifice among many standardizing groups. And it could, along with the basic research aspects of standards, provide one rationale for increased governmental involvement. These issues are developed further in Chapters 3, 7, and 8.

But standardization generally involves what might loosely be termed "selective incentives,"[16] meaning that rewards vary somewhat directly with members contribution toward the attainment of the common goal. In the case of standards, while they might benefit all group members, the degree of benefit can largely depend on the exact standard chosen. Thus standard steel specifications probably helped all automobile concerns, but since there were sunk costs (capital and knowledge) and possible change-over problems, it mattered what exact standards were selected. This would be true, also, to varying extents for automobile parts standards, railway gauge standards, screw thread standards, etc. Therefore, if standards are going to be written, a firm may well have an incentive to be on the standards writing committee. Since for many standards the potential absolute benefits or costs are related to firm size, while the cost of participating in the standardizing process is often independent of size, we should suspect (with Mancur Olsen) that large firms would dominate the standards writing process. Which they do. More on this in Chapters 7 and 8.

The possible problem that Olsen foresees of underinvestment in collective good provision is also alleviated in standards-making by the existence of organizations, principally engineering societies and trade associations, that serve a variety of functions, only one of which is writing standards. These organizations, of course, may develop goals of their own, one of which may become extensive standardization. It still remains true, however, that because of negotiation and bargaining strategies and problems many worthwhile standards may not be produced. All of which is only to illustrate the point emphasized here, that there is probably no automatic mechanism which assures some proper amount of standardization.

3. In the real world, the major impetus for intercompany standards

seems usually to come from the buyers side. Sellers are more likely to oppose standards, perhaps because they lessen the competitive advantage of firms with established reputations for quality, or merely increase buyer information or simply decrease managerial perogatives. Buyers possessing power, either as individuals or by acting conjointly, must then often impose the standards on sellers. The SAE-standard steels example provides one illustration. The fact that almost all voluntary standards in the United States are for producers' rather than consumers' goods is most indicative. Chapters 3, 5, and especially 7 focus on the whole question of the impetus for standards creation. Let us just conclude here by noting that the absence of voluntary standards for final goods is largely due to the difficulty of organizing the vast, latent consumer interest.

Part II

Standards for Uniformity

The next three chapters examine industrywide standards for uniformity. The goal is to give an account of the role played by such standards in our economy, and to relate the emergence of these standards to characteristics of market structure. This book classifies standards for uniformity into two main groupings—those standards where product interchangeability is the main consideration and those standards where it is not. The former generally involves two or more distinct parts or products that work together as one (tires and rims, staples and staplers). The latter standards usually concern the simplification of a single product (nails, paint brushes, milk bottles). In the real world, of course, there is no such easy dichotomy, and after a description of single product standards for uniformity in Chapter 3, Chapter 4 discusses a variety of standards not definitely categorizable as either/or. In Chapter 5 the focus is on standards involving interchangeability. The economics of tying proves quite helpful in this final analysis. Comments are scattered throughout the chapter concerning possible major economic effects of the presence or absence of standards for uniformity.

Chapter Three

Single Product Standards

The standards for uniformity examined first are those dealing with a single product, where interchangeability is not at issue. Examples of such simplification include the conscious reduction of the variety of paint brushes in the 1920s from 480 kinds to 138, of tacks from 428 varieties to 181, of files from 1,350 to 496.[1] The recent reductions in package varieties under the Fair Packaging and Labelling Act provide further illustrations of single product standards for uniformity.

The principal benefits from such standards lie largely in two areas: improved information, particularly to buyers, and lower costs if purchases are focused on a few varieties, allowing economies of scale in production or distribution. We will first examine the possible economy of scale gains due to these standards.

ECONOMY OF SCALE BENEFITS

Intercompany standards might prove useful if the average costs of produc...g particular varieties decrease over a range, and the purchases of individual buyers are not large enough to realize the full economies. If, for example, small buyers are ordering varieties sufficiently different that they prohibit scale economies, standards could help coordinate their purchases and possibly reduce costs. Appendix A uses pay-off matrices to formalize a number of such cases.

When individual buyers are large in the market it is not normally necessary for them to coordinate intercompany purchases in order to permit economies of scale in production (or often, in distribution). Of course, when buyers are few in number, coordination among them is usually easiest and standards are likely to emerge could they prove beneficial.

When sellers are large in the market they can often be relied on to offer the option of a few varieties at lowered cost. Small sellers may have more difficulty in unilaterally limiting variety. It may be costly to discover what varieties can be successfully eliminated, and for the small concern, *ceteris paribus*, a selected alternative must be acceptable to a larger percentage of its customers to permit all scale economies. The risks of unilateral reduction may sometimes simply outweigh the potential benefits.

The principal situation where there *might* be a real need for intercompany standards to secure economy benefits is when both sellers and (purchases of) buyers are small. This is often the case when atomistic buyers face atomistic sellers. Unfortunately large numbers also make the requisite coordination needed for standardization most difficult. In such circumstances public action may prove helpful, and indeed it has been upon industries characterized by low buyer and seller concentration that the U.S. government has focused its simplification efforts.

Before discussing actual government aided simplification efforts, it should be noted that sellers may sometimes oppose industrywide variety reduction, even when it permits economies of scale. Sellers, for example, may be reluctant to relinquish captive markets. Thus the SAE parts standards, which limited the dependence of the automobile assembler on specific sellers, might not have been welcomed by particular suppliers. Such a situation, however, fundamentally involves interchangeability standards, and will be discussed in that Chapter of the book.

Sellers may also oppose standards if they increase buyer information. Thus the early steel producers seemed quite content to forego the cost reductions allowed by large-scale production in order to maintain the advantages of uninformed buyers and product differentiation. The steel example, though, involves quality standards. Yet it must be stressed that standards and the standardizing process itself generally increase information, and this may prove detrimental to certain interests. The information aspects of standards will be analyzed at length in various sections of the book.

Historically in the United States, simplification activity has reached its peak during wartime. In World War I, for example, the War Industries Board pushed for variety reduction in an effort to conserve on materials and productive capacity. Concentrating largely on consumer goods, the board eliminated 5,500 styles of rubber footwear, cut tire varieties from 287 to 32, and reduced the number of washing machine models from 445 to 18. In all, conservation orders went out to some three hundred industry groups.[2]

Herbert Hoover was impressed by this World War I product simplification. In 1921, as president of the Federated American Engineering Societies, he authorized studies to determine the extent of waste in industry. The report examined six typical industries—building trades, men's ready-made clothing, boots and shoes, printing, metal trades and textile manufacturing. It claimed that preventable waste accounted for from 29 to 64 per cent of costs, and that billions could be saved annually by industrywide standardization and simplification.[3]

The report stimulated another wave of simplification, this time voluntary and organized by industry groups. Indeed, many present-day trade associations date from this period; they were organized initially to draw up standards.[4] Incomplete statistics indicate the growing importance of these activities throughout the 1920s. In 1926, for example, 69 trade associations reported expenditures for standardizing programs. By 1928 the number had risen to 240.[5]

When Hoover became Secretary of Commerce, he established a Division of Simplified Practice, and in 1927 he greatly amplified its activities. The function of the division was to cooperate with producers, distributors, and consumers to help eliminate needless varieties of products. Examples of commodities simplified under the auspices of the Department of Commerce include beds, shotgun shells, hotel chinaware, paint brushes, nails, files, and business forms.[6] A noteworthy example of simplification occurred when the paving brick manufacturers met in Washington, with Hoover as a principal speaker. The firms discovered that together they produced sixty-six varieties of brick. In less than six hours they agreed to eliminate all but eleven.[7]

Now mere reduction in variety is not sufficient for a "standard for uniformity" as the term is used in this book. If, for example, eleven brick firms each manufactured six unique varieties, and after joint deliberation they each eliminated five varieties from their product lines, there would still be no product uniformity. Standards for uniformity require that separate firms, forming a substantial segment of the industry, decide to make products that are identical in certain important (often dimensional) characteristics.

On the other hand, suppose the eleven brick manufacturers were each making all sixty-six varieties, and they collectively agreed to eliminate fifty-five and concentrate on the same eleven. Here (perhaps implicit) standards for uniformity existed before collective action, but increased "standardization" has clearly occurred. Maybe this case should be called something like pure Simplification, with a capital S.

In the general case, of course, collective variety reduction makes the products of separate suppliers more similar or uniform. Without further information, this book assumes that this will be the effect of any simplification.

The large majority of those industries whose products were simplified under Department of Commerce procedures during the 1920s seem to have had low buyer concentration. Often the purchasing industry was atomistic (chinaware for hotels), or the product was used by various industries (business forms), or bought by final consumers (beds). If the hypothesis that buyers usually provide the impetus for standardization is correct, it was proper that these industries receive the bulk of the government's attention. In those areas most difficult for buyers to act collectively, the government could provide the most help. It makes good sense too that simplification efforts in World Wars I and II were focused on consumer goods industries. And it is not surprising that variety proliferation reappeared when the mandatory controls were lifted.[8]

A goodly number of products simplified by the new Division of Simplified Practice seem also to have involved industries with many small sellers. To the extent that our previous brief analysis applies, governmental help in the standardizing process could prove most beneficial in these industries characterized by low seller as well as buyer concentration ratios. A prime example here is the lumber industry. Users are many and diverse, and high transport cost, resource location, and the available technology has kept the seller side relatively atomistic. There was an enormous number of sizes and varieties of lumber in the 20s, and substantial cost savings were possible, primarily in transport and storage, if the industry could agree on standards for uniformity.

In 1922 Hoover hosted the first of three industrywide conferences. By the final conference virtually every affected party (save for final consumers) was being represented. Buyers were represented by the Association of Wood-Using Industries and the National Association of Purchasing Agents. Lumber retailers and wholesalers had delegates from their respective national and state societies. Lumber producers were represented by the National Lumber Manufacturers Association along with more specialized associations representing the Northern hemlock producers, the Southern cypress, the California redwood, the North Carolina pine, etc. The American Institute of Architects, the Associated General Contractors, and the American Society of Civil Engineers were also in attendance.[9] At this conference it was agreed to reduce the number of lumber yard sizes by 60 per cent. Of the $300 million figure often cited by Hoover in the 1920s as documented annual savings due to Commerce simplification activities, the reduction in lumber yard varieties accounted for $250 million.[10]

It should be realized that to have dimensional standards for uniformity there needs to be common agreement on terminology and measurement. For example, what exactly is a "2 by 4"? Would it be 2" by 4" when the lumber is green or dried, uncut, sawed, planed or what? What are the acceptable tolerances? (Presently, a 2 by 4 has no connection with 2" by 4".) In the lumber industry, terminology and measurement agreements have been significant in their own right, and are discussed further as quality standards in Chapter 7.

We have argued that intercompany standards are most needed to permit scale economies in markets characterized by atomism on both sides, but in such circumstances industrywide collective action is difficult and standards may not emerge. The lumber industry illustrated such a situation where governmental action proved helpful. The analysis thus far has implicitly assumed that industrywide cost reductions are normally desired. This seems usually, but not necessarily universally the case for sellers, or buyers of intermediate goods.

Where there are high entry barriers, industrywide standards that cut costs can permit long-run increases in industry profits, and would be generally welcomed, though there may be some dynamic problems. In atomistic markets with low entry barriers the conclusion is less clear. In the long run, of course, "perfect" competition means no excess profits. In the short run, however, before new firms can enter the industry, cost reductions can affect the profits of existing firms, and there is no reason why such gains or losses will ever be offset. Collectively, then, existing small firms may have incentives to promote or impede standards that uniformly decrease costs.

If the across-the-board cost reductions affect only fixed costs, then a firm's average cost will fall, but the marginal cost remains unchanged. Industry short-run supply is thus unaffected, as is price. The short-run profits of all firms increase, since average cost falls while price holds constant. Existing firms may then have an incentive to promote such standards—say via their trade association—assuming of course that the benefits are greater than the costs of standardizing.

If fixed costs remain unchanged, and marginal costs decrease, the effect on the short-run profit of established firms is largely determined by the industry elasticity of demand. If demand is very elastic, price will fall less than average cost, and short-run profits are likely. There is the perverse possibility, however, that with a very inelastic industry demand combined with firm average cost curves that shift right as well as down, prices could fall precipitously—more than average costs—and profits could actually decrease in the short run.

Interindustry competition appears important in affecting the incentives for intercompany standards permitting economies of scale. When there are good substitutes for a product, demand will be elastic, and firms should generally be happy to see cost cuts, even across the entire industry. Where industry demand is inelastic, the conclusion is less certain. In Chapter 7 there will again be a discussion of the impact of interindustry competition on collective decisions.

The analysis has indicated that even atomistic firms should generally welcome across-the-board cost reductions. There are also other incentives, of course, in promoting industrywide standards that allow scale economies. The small auto concerns, for example, finally created SAE parts standards because the standards helped them combat intra-industry rivals; in this case it lessened the competitive advantage of the emerging large-scale enterprise. In the lumber example, the standards for uniformity primarily cut *shipping* costs. This meant that the price of lumber *plus* transportation would fall, increasing the demand for lumber, and improving the short-run profit position of established concerns.

In the lumber example, the individual small shipper probably did not have the knowledge, and it was too risky for a single firm to select and promote its own standard where no consensus had yet emerged. Furthermore, if one succeeded in creating a widely followed standard, *all* shippers might reap the benefit. Collectively, the atomistic shippers, like the lumber firms themselves, might have had great difficulty in getting together to hammer out beneficial standards. A monopolist shipper, on the other hand, has more information and under most assumptions a strong incentive to cut industry costs. His profits could increase dramatically in both the short and long run. Thus even our own post office may be willing and able to push magazines toward dimensional uniformity, whereas a more competitive industry might not. The analysis becomes quite Schumpeterian.

The point to be made here is that monopolists and oligopolists (or monopsonies and oligopsonies) often do not need industrywide standards to gain scale economies. But when they do, their small numbers alone mean they generally have greater ability to create workable ones.

INFORMATION BENEFITS

A second and probably more important benefit of single product standards for uniformity is in the area of information. While the long analysis of the economies of information is reserved for Chapter 6, a number of aspects of standards and information will be discussed here.

It should first be emphasized that knowledge about the product is increased during the standardization process itself, when information is exchanged and possibly research done. The coordination role of standardization is partly the provision of information, information that the individual seller might be unable to cheaply discover on what varieties could be successfully eliminated.

Some product standards result merely from the provision of information across the industry. As part of its information gathering and dissemination functions, for example, a trade association may try to discover the sizes and specifications of items currently being purchased. Some associations provide such information to the industry in terms of Recommended Standards. Take, for example, the Paper Stationery and Tablet Manufacturers Association. From its research, it recommends that typewriter tablets sizes should be 8½ x 11 inches or 8½ x 13, that composition books should be 8½ x 7, 10 x 8, or 10½ x 8. While the association does not strenuously urge that its recommendations be followed, the provision of such information since the 1930s has undoubtedly helped promote standards for uniformity. (The National Bureau of Standards was aiding simplification efforts in this industry in the 1920s.) This is the whole purpose of the recommendations, to help achieve cost savings, via simplification, the focal points for coordination being (what the association says are) the most commonly purchased varieties. To quote from the bulletin:

> This publication has been developed to avert waste of material, time and money. Major factors of waste include unnecessary duplications of raw and finished inventories, multiple manufacturing runs, and frequent machine changes, where sizes and other specifications are only slightly and unnecessarily different from those already accepted as standard. The voluntary adoption of these standards by manufacturers, distributors and users should result in a considerable amount of saving.[11]

Simplification can also permit, over time, a greater accumulation of experience to be built up concerning those varieties remaining on the market. Standard items, for example, are known to be dependable, having been subject to considerable and various tests. Variety reduction can also immediately ease consumers comparison shopping problems. The remainder of this section describes simplification in the container industry, focusing on the possible pricing information benefits for final consumers.

The Container Industry

The government has long been involved with simplification activities in the container industry. Sometimes the purpose was to improve consumer information, more usually it was to reduce costs, and often it was war related. At the request of the National Preservers Association, for example, in the early thirties the National Bureau of Standards conducted a survey to reveal the sales of various sized jelly jars. Here the government was providing collectively useful information. In 1932, under the auspices of the bureau, manufacturers, distributors, and retailers agreed to reduce the variety of preserve jars from forty sizes to nine, jelly glasses from twenty-five sizes to seven, and applebutter jars from six sizes to four. The National Bureau of Standards promulgated similar simplified practice recommendations for milk and cream bottles, mayonnaise jars, cottage cheese and sour cream containers.[12]

The World War II conservation program helped push variety reduction in the olive and cherry packing industries. The maraschino cherry case illustrates the possible benefits of governmental simplification activities. With fewer varieties, the costs of producing cherry jars dropped due to the benefits of longer production runs—fewer changes, less idle equipment, and simplified inspection. Packers costs also dropped substantially.[13] But without governmental assistance it is not at all clear that any individual or group had enough incentive and ability to promote industrywide variety and cost reductions. It is interesting to note that such standards are not universally followed; that while use of odd-sized containers may increase costs, it can also differentiate the product and increase eye-appeal.[14]

Most recently the bureau has been given responsibility to promote standards for uniformity in containers under the Fair Labelling and Packaging Act. The purpose is to reduce variety for ease of comparison shopping. The theory behind the simplification portions of the FLPA might run something like this:

Suppose goods come packaged, and the weight of the product (such as flour) is of primary interest to the consumer. Within certain broad ranges, however, he is relatively indifferent as to the exact weight. He does not particularly care whether a package is 12½ or 13½ ounces, but he would like small, medium, and large packages to exist. Now individual sellers can package the product in any of a virtually limitless number of possible sizes. Economies of scale dictate that they choose only a few sizes, and for simplicity we might assume they select one from each of the three broad ranges. There is no reason, of course, that different sellers will pick the exact same sizes. (Indeed, they may have reason to choose different sizes.) Nor is an individual seller prevented from varying his sizes. If the information directly available to the consumer is only package pack and size, he is required to do a lot of arithmetic to determine the relative prices per pound. This can be difficult, time-consuming, and costly, especially when many items are being purchased. Studies continually find that even intelligent consumers are unable to point out the low price item.[15]

There are, in effect, externalities in one's purchases. This seems a general phenomenon. For example, one family's decision to eat at a particular restaurant may increase another's wait-in-line costs; or one student's refusal to attend Harvard basketball games may reduce fan noise, excitement, and others' enjoyment of the game. In the case at hand, by buying dissimilar sizes, consumers increase each other's shopping costs. Consumers might thus be better off with only a few "standard" size packages. But collectively, manufacturers have little incentive to provide these. Indeed many, especially high price, sellers prefer to keep price comparisons difficult and to limit price competition. Consumers may find no way of effectively coordinating their purchases to indicate a preference for standards. Thus, even for a perfectly homogeneous product, a large number of sizes may emerge, each able to "pay its own way." Yet consumers would prefer a number of these eliminated. The problem is that, individually, they have no way of determining which ones. Since consumers have not established an association capable of adequately representing them (the Mancor Olsen problem), the government could play a constructive role by coordinating demand or forcing simplification.

The FLPA hearings were held because of numerous consumer complaints.[16] Here we have another example of the general phenomenon of buyers providing the impetus for standardization. At the numerous hearings every consumer spokesmen strongly supported the bills, while virtually every producing interest argued against them. A part of the producers opposition undoubtedly stemmed from the simple desire to maintain discretionary power and their fear of arbitrary governmental action.

The idea behind FLPA simplification was not new. In the United States many states have long limited the number of acceptable sizes (weight or volume) for certain basic commodities. Sale of packaged bread, for example, is often permitted only in half pound multiples, butter and margarine might be limited to one-quarter, one-half, and one pound weights, and milk containers to simple fractions of the gallon.[17] In Great Britain, the government has simplified sizes for forty categories of staples.[18]

Alcohol containers have often been the subject of regulation. In the 1950s, for example, when national breweries introduced the 10 ounce can in certain markets as a means of competing against cheaper local beers, many state governments passed restricting legislation. The issue here was, in part, deceptive packaging–the feat that consumers might initially mistake the 10 ounce size for the usual 12. So Florida, for example, now only permits packaged beer to be sold in the 8, 12, 16 or 32 ounce container. Other states imposed tax arrangements discriminatory to the "odd-sized" package. In California, on the other hand, a strange tax structure has induced brewers to use 11 and 15 ounce containers, which receive favorable treatment compared to the regular sizes.[19]

Bottles of hard alcohol are often restricted to the quart, fifth, and other "popular" sizes. That this does not completely inhibit package innovation can readily be seen in the Yuletide liquor displays. The mandatory simplification here is based on notions similar to the FLPA, that the costs to the consumer of having fewer sizes to choose among is more than compensated by the facilitation of price comparisons and lessened likelihood of deception.

FLPA simplification provisions, however, have not proved particularly beneficial.[20] There are a number of reasons for this. For items that are not themselves the sole final good, simplification may not make much sense. Thus consumers want enough cake mix to make a cake (when adding a whole number of eggs) and trying to standardize heterogeneous mixes by weight or volume would be silly. More important, many manufacturers use the same packaging machinery for a number of products (either in different markets, as canned peas and canned corn, or differentiated products in the same market, as Kellogg's K and Rice Krispies). To force package standardization *might* increase packaging costs, or slack fill if different density items are packaged in identical containers. But basically, FLPA simplification has not proved immensely helpful because there is no effective enforcement (odd size toothpaste tubes still abound), the standards often permit size proliferation (there are 72 standard candy weights, 56 cookie weights, 37 approved packages of mixed nuts), and frequently prohibit vertical price comparisons. Dry detergent packages, for example are standardized at 6, 20, 49, 84, 171, and 257 ounces.[21] Finally, a simpler, less controversial method of facilitating price comparisons is at last making some headway. This is unit price information. Why it has taken so long for unit pricing to catch-on is a question for interesting speculation.

To speculate briefly: Supermarkets, with low prices and large variety, seem one logical place for unit pricing to begin. Supermarkets provide a whole host of heterogeneous services to shoppers, and if they are to compete in terms of "gimmicks," they should prefer ones which would promote repeat shopping–such as trading stamps–and receive little flak from manufacturers. With half a book of green stamps, a customer has an investment and is less likely to buy in Plain Stamp territory. Unit price competition however, like price competition for a homogeneous product, can be matched immediately. Even without recognized interdependence, of course, many supermarkets might have believed the small cost for unit pricing was not worth the benefit. Most probably didn't think about it.

PROBLEMS

The discussion thus far has somewhat assumed that standards are beneficial from the viewpoint of society. This does generally seem to be the case for pure single product standards for uniformity, especially if they are voluntary. This is not to imply that voluntary standards are superior to mandatory ones, but only that their voluntary nature lessens the likelihood of harmful effects. Sellers sometimes have incentives to distinguish themselves, to differentiate their products, and with voluntary standards for uniformity they can usually do so. The list is long of those standards no longer followed.

The problem generally is not one of too many standards, but too few. Some discussion is required, however, of those cases where voluntary standards for uniformity may possibly have deleterious effects.

A general potential problem with all existing standards is that they may impede improvement. For standards for uniformity, this usually means the movement to a wider or superior standard for uniformity! Such problems are rare for single product standards, more likely for standards where interchangeability is important. Examples are record player speeds, and typewriter keyboards. Record player speeds and typewriter keyboards involve superior and inferior standards for uniformity. Two attempts were made to displace the 78 rpm phonograph, and both succeeded and failed, so record players now operate at three speeds. While the new standards were superior to the old, consumers were unwilling to scrap their 78 rpm collections. So manufacturers make turntables for their use.[22] Typewriters are single products, but the exact nature of the keyboard affects the interchangeability of typists skills. This is discussed further in subsequent pages. Improved keyboards have been unable to replace the old standard.

More general illustrations include the difficulty of changing from the customary system of measurement to the metric, from 120 to 220 voltage lines. The fundamental concept here is that while some standard for uniformity is better than none, when trying to achieve a more universally acceptable, or a superior standard, it is often better to start from a state of disarray. It would be easier, for example, to establish an international screw thread standard if competing national standards were not already being followed.

Looking at instances where it would be preferable to have *no* standard for uniformity, rather than merely a more universally acceptable standard, we should generally find problems only when the standards are created by sellers (or by buyers who are subsequent sellers). If final consumers wrote standards (e.g., FLPA), even if there were some costs (changeover problems, slack fill, etc.) the collective benefits should outweigh these costs or the standards would not be created. There may, of course, be problems if consumers are ignorant, irrational, or there are spill-over effects to others inadequately represented in the standardization process. The discussion here ignores all the "public finance" and distribution complexities.

When sellers write single product standards for uniformities, there are two major problems: the witholding of desired variety from the market and the facilitation of illegal activity. The first problem is perhaps more interesting theoretically, the latter appears more prevalent in the real world.

Assume a profit-maximizing seller is considering introducing a new line or variety. He should not do so if the revenue brought in is less than the cost. Now revenue should be net revenue, subtracting losses on other lines due to the new variety. Many varieties that in accounting terms appear to be "paying their own way" might better be eliminated (or never introduced). If the seller in question is a member of a tight-knit oligopoly with high mutually recognized interdependence, he should also consider the effect of his actions on rival firms. They might view the new line as an act of aggression, or he might simply expect quick but passive imitation, with possible detriment for all. Standards here might help prevent the problem, but are probably not even needed. Furthermore, while real world examples are not rare, they generally involve decidedly inferior and superior lines (if there were standards, they would be really quality standards). Thus the airlines were long reluctant to introduce coach class, and domestic automobile manufacturers balked at introducing the small car.[23]

A more common but related problem caused by standards for uniformity is that they can expedite oligopolistic collusion. The principal illegal activity in question is price-fixing, or at least this has always been the focus of antitrust activity involving standards.[24] The role of standards for uniformity is that since price is price per something, by creating a few standard "somethings," price-fixing may be facilitated, and industry self-enforcement made easier. It can be argued, for example, that the many implicit standards for uniformity for tobacco products perform just such a function. Lengths of cigarettes, numbers to a carton, and cartons to a pack are all similar industrywide. These uniformities are not forced by technology, and undoubtedly help enforce the price parallelism of this highly oligopolistic industry. It is illuminating that in the 1930s, when the market share of the Big 3 fell markedly, many of the uniformities briefly disappeared.[25]

CONCLUDING COMMENTS

Single product standards for uniformity can provide information and economy of scale benefits. Intercompany standards are normally not needed to permit scale economies, but when they are, it is usually when both buyers and sellers are small. In markets characterized by atomism on both sides, however, the coordination needed for standardization is most difficult to obtain. In the past, the government has tried to aid in such situations and, especially in the 1920s, helped create some beneficial standards.

Single product standards for uniformity may yield information benefits when buyers' purchases are so small that even calculating unit prices may represent a significant cost. Unless threatened by public action, sellers have little joint incentive to ease consumers' price comparison problems (except as a by-product of their attempts to facilitate oligopolistic price coordination). The government thus initiated the Fair Labelling and Packaging Act, in part to help the unorganized, atomistic final consumer comparison shop. Success in this area has been, at best, questionable, and unit pricing is beginning to provide a less troublesome substitute.

While this chapter has discussed only standards for goods, it is rewarding to consider some "non-product uniformities." Some are simply coordination games, as the night retail stores remain open, or the standard forty hour work week. (This latter, pushed by unions in the 1930s, has become somewhat mandatory since it is written into overtime laws.)[26] The locational clustering of certain markets has characteristics similar to product uniformities, with sometimes similar problems of moving to a superior area (standard).

Industrywide price uniformities are interesting examples of "standards," and we will conclude this section with a brief discussion of some. Our coinage system, and sometimes the use of vending machines, cause many inexpensive items to standardize at 5, 10 or 15¢. Thus, in the past, Hershey and Mr. Goodbars appear to have been standardized at 10¢, the size of the bars varying with raw material prices.[27] Similar examples of price standardization include chewing gum and newspapers. Inflation has eventually shifted most of these standards. Competition and Consumer Behavior have combined to produce a number of interesting uniformities. Retail gasoline prices, for example, have become stuck with a .9 cent ending. Prices for packaged candy customarily have 9¢ endings. These are considered the "magic prices," and there is clearly packaging-to-price, rather than vice versa. The practice of packaging-to-price was one of the reasons business was afraid of FLPA. Once uniform price endings have been established in an industry there is sometimes an incentive to break convention to distinguish one's product. Thus an unfamiliar $ .31 or $ .73 ending might carry a strong implication of discounting, or a genuine bargain. A point to be made here, emphasized by Carolyn Bell,[28] is that prices play not only a rationing function in the economy, but, among other things, serve to create an impression.

Chapter Four

Intermediate Standards

There are a wide variety of standards for uniformity that do not fit nicely into the simple "single product standards"–"standards for interchangeability" division used in this book. Four general groups of such standards are discussed in this chapter.

1. measurements standards, especially for clothing (pantyhose sizes);
2. standards for the interchangeability of people and machines (typewriter keyboard);
3. product interchangeability standards involving a single product (bricks);
4. standards, often informal, for products used or sold in dispensing machines (paper towels).

MEASUREMENT STANDARDS

Shopping for clothing can clearly be facilitated by a standard system of sizing. It is most helpful, for example, if a size 44 T-shirt from Manufacturer X is dimensionally similar to a 44 from Manufacturer Y. There are externalities in the situation, and competition will not insure the creation of a system of beneficial standards. Standards are normally quite useful here because even with effective demand for size information, firms rarely arise to provide it (to tell that Manufacturer X's size 44 is almost equivalent to Manufacturer Y's size M). There is some cost (though small in this case) of initially discovering the relationships, and since this information lacks appropriability, there may be little incentive for any firm to do the initial work. If the relationships are discovered, and the extra cost of giving the information to an additional person is close to zero, then a positive price on it may inefficiently exclude some shoppers. And if the information is not provided at the point of sale, there are problems of losing it, remembering to bring it along, etc. Such information could be provided by the retailer, but like unit pricing, rarely has been. There is much more on information in Chapter 6.

Collective action is usually required to create size standards. Individual manufacturers may welcome, oppose, or be indifferent to such industrywide standards. Even assuming they all desire standards, voluntary creation requires agreement, and has costs of its own, as well as necessitating some change-over costs. Since total benefits greatly exceed total costs for at least some standardization, governmental help in expediting standards writing may be eminently justified.

In the 1930s and 1940s, with the help of the National Bureau of Standards, men's pajamas and boys garments were successfully standardized. National Bureau assistance in standardization has often consisted of data collection as well as general facilitation of agreement regarding the definition and minimum measurements for various aspects of clothing. After a survey of male measurements, for example, size A pajama coats were standardized with minimum length of 30", chest of 43", armhole of 20", sleeve length of 32", etc.[1] In Canada, standards have only quite recently been written for children's garments. The Canadian government, at the request of the Consumers Association of Canada, began such work in the fifties, but it was not until 1969 that Canada Standard Sizes for children's clothing were finally promulgated.[2]

In the 1970s, standards were produced in the United States for the pantyhose industry. The National Association of Hosiery Manufacturers ran a huge computerized study of women's measurements, and from this developed a standard sizing chart for women. The survey seems to have helped individual manufacturers create better fitting pantyhose,[3] as well as to promote agreement on standard sizes.

INTERCHANGEABILITY OF PEOPLE AND MACHINES

Some single product standards for uniformity are primarily concerned with the interchangeability of people, allowing one to more fully utilize the knowledge and experience acquired in one area or with one manufacturer's product. (Standard garment sizes have this effect.) A number of early federal automobile safety standards are designed for this purpose. Automatic gears are now standardized with neutral between Reverse and Drive, in part to help prevent unaccustomed drivers from accidently going the wrong way. Dashboards are to be more uniform to help drivers find the right knob—so that at night you don't turn *off* the headlights when trying to turn *on* the windshield wipers, etc.[4]

Forklift trucks are almost completely standardized so that drivers can be trained quickly to operate the truck of any manfuacturer. Previously, some lift trucks had left-hand drive, some right-hand drive. Acceleration was sometimes controlled by the right foot, sometimes by the left hand. Different trucks had different levers with similar functions. With standard trucks, drivers are more "interchangeable."[5]

Traffic lights have been standardized so that red, yellow, and green are standard colors, are at similar heights and locations, and mean pretty much the same thing throughout the United States. It would be of benefit if some state driving laws reached a high level of national uniformity.

A quite interesting example of an informal standard for people-interchangeability is the typewriter keyboard. It makes a great deal of sense to have some keyboard uniformity, especially since while people can be multilingual they cannot be "multidigital." The current keyboard, however, was basically the first, and is far from the best. The present keyboard was designed in 1873 with the purpose of keeping keys used together as far apart as possible since the key return mechanism worked quite slowly. But clashing type bars are no longer a problem, and other keyboards have been proven markedly superior. Yet acting individually, society has been unable to change to a better system, even though a single focal-point alternative, the Dvorak system, has stood in readiness for over forty years.[6]

SINGLE PRODUCT INTERCHANGEABILITY STANDARDS

Some single product standards for uniformity are largely for *product* interchangeability. Brick simplification can be seen in this light. For a purchaser, it is especially beneficial when replacing old bricks to have an industrywide standard since then there is less likelihood of being locked into a single producer, and competitive bidding is facilitated. The government, as a major brick buyer (particularly at one time for street paving), has been instrumental in promoting uniform standards. It is reported, for example, that in Boston, after the 1689 fire, standards were published and makers of nonstandard bricks were punished—by a term in the stocks![7]

Railway gauges provide another example of single product standards for interchangeability. End-to-end railroads usually have clear incentives for gauge uniformities, and in most countries, with a large amount of governmental involvement, a single dimensional standard has emerged. A bumper height standard for cars would be another example of beneficial uniformity, but one which does not exist. Manufacturers have had little incentive to create one, the unorganized consumer has been unable to impose one, and the government, unfortunately, has not played a role. While consumers generally would like uniform bumper heights to decrease damage expenses, individually they can neither write nor enforce a standards, and collectively they have thus far been unable to get together.

STANDARDS FOR DISPENSERS

Some products are dimensionally uniform because they are often used or sold in uniform dispensing machines. Paper towels, for example, come in an enormous variety of lengths, colors, number of sheets per roll, plys, etc. Yet virtually all are eleven inches wide, in order to fit the commonly available dispenser.[8] Toilet paper is all 4.5" wide (as well, intriguingly, as 4.5" long). Even comic book sizes are uniform, its trade association believes, because the display racks are.[9] How such dispensers have become uniform is, unfortunately, not entirely clear. Yet once established, the "standard," like most of those discussed in this chapter, becomes very difficult to change. In discussing products and dispensers, we are very close to two product standards for uniformity, to which we now turn.

Chapter Five

Interchangeability Standards

There are a great many uniformity standards between two (or more) products or parts that promote interchangeability. Examples include tires and rims, pipe flanges and fittings, nuts and bolts, shafting pins and washers, guns and ammunition, records and record players, cameras and film, flashlights and batteries, bulbs and lamp sockets, even beds and sheets. A particularly interesting example of "standards" for interchangeability comes from the Color Association of the United States. A primary function of this association is to help coordinate, in terms of color, different segments of the consumer market—millinery, shoes, gloves with ready-to-wear; wallpaper, paint, draperies with carpets; glasswear with table linen; shower curtains with towels and bathroom accessories. "The wrong colors could be fatal."[1] While the "in" colors continually change, the association provides Standard Color Cards (specifications) to ease communication and pinpoint the required shade. (The association is principally helpful for merchandise manufactured abroad to be exported to the United States.)

BENEFITS

Interchangeability standards for uniformity can permit economies of scale and improve information. They help limit variety, like single product standards, and thus allow longer production runs. They may reduce comparative shopping problems, and can decrease other search costs. Color Association Standards, for example, should lessen the color problems of foreign fashion manufacturers. For the final consumer in the United States, it certainly makes life easier to have a few standard bed sizes—especially when buying fitted sheets, or a few standard phonograph speeds—especially when buying records for a present.

For gift-giving, it probably makes some difference whether or not dual-products are standardized. One suspects that lack of standards decrease

37

single item presents of pen cartridges, razor blades, or candle stick holders, while standards increase the likelihood of giving records or blankets.

The most important benefit of interchangeability standards is that they widen markets, increasing alternative sources of supply. Because of standards, a consumer with a flashlight in not "locked-in" to one or two battery manufacturers. Many battery manufacturers can economically produce the standard sizes, knowing that demand for them will be high, since flashlight producers are making flashlights so that standard batteries will fit. And flashlight producers are busy making standard flashlights, for demand here will be greatest, since few people want flashlights if they can't easily get batteries.

In a competitive world, with perfect information and foresight, existing alternative supply sources may not be necessary since buyers take into account *total* price (including the price of the complementary item, plus future replacement needs) when making an initial purchase. But in the real world of business failures, delivery delays, quality changes—in a world without perfect foresight and with imperfect competition—alternative supply sources can provide great benefits. Buyers, for example, may be willing to pay to keep open their short-run options. Standards often prove a most efficient way of doing this, In a real sense, then, interchangeability standards can play a role similar to *insurance*.

Standards, by widening markets, thus tend to reduce certain risks. Yet while wider markets generally have socially beneficial effects, they can increase the risk of crime. Standardized bike parts, for example, should increase the potential use of stolen bikes. There supposedly was talk at one time of making government light bulbs screw the wrong way—to decrease the profitability of theft!

The fact that standards for interchangeability provide information and widen markets means they generally serve to enhance entry. Thus a potential light bulb manufacturer is probably more likely to enter the market knowing that if he follows existing standards his bulbs will fit virtually all existing lamps, as well as function properly on existing voltages. In some sense, a uniform lamp base widens his immediate potential market, as well as making retaliation by existing suppliers somewhat less likely. Contrast, for example, the above situation to one with fifteen different types of major lamp bases, with one or two manufacturers supplying total needs for each "submarket." (Actually, of course, it is questionable that the lamp base would ever be the major characteristic delineating principal submarkets.) Differing national standards for uniformity can, of course, *raise* entry barriers against foreign competition.

Overall, present uniformity standards for interchangeability generally have beneficial effects. A consumer, for example, using an Ansco film in a Graflex camera resting on a Burke and James tripod using a Wollensax lens, a Kodak color filter and a G.E. exposure meter, owes it all, I have read, to standardization.[2]

PROBLEMS

Potential problems arising from interchangeability standards are greatest when sellers create the standards. Like all standards for uniformity, interchangeability standards might help suppliers to collectively withhold some desired variety from the market, or might facilitate illegal price-fixing schemes. However, few voluntary interchangeability standards come to mind which have been detrimental to society in these ways. The principal real world problems from such standards stem from the possibility that they might stifle innovation.

If two complementary industries composed of separate firms each produce standard, and interchangeable, products it may be more difficult for any one producer to break away with a radical departure. If safety razors and blades were made by different manufacturers, for example, and there was great interchangeability, it might have been harder for a single razor company to have introduced the injector or double-blade concept. In the rapidly changing computer field, the National Bureau of Standards has recently declined to write interface standards on the ground that they would retard innovation.[3] On the other hand, while standards might have deterred innovation in some instances, to the extent that they actually widen markets and increase competition, we *might* expect them to generally promote progressiveness, especially concerning product aspects not intimately connected with interchangeability.

INTERCHANGEABILITY STANDARDS
AND MARKET STRUCTURE

If buyers are large in the market and few in number, they can usually agree to coordinate their purchases to create the interchangeability standards they find mutually beneficial. When buyers are small and numerous and have difficulty coordinating their actions, the structure of the sellers side of the market is generally crucial in determining if beneficial standards are written. The key market variables seem to be whether manufacturers are producing both (or all) of the conjoint products, and if so, whether any such firm possesses market power in at least one of the lines.

When firms are not producing both the conjoint products, interchangeability standards can decrease their dependence on other specific suppliers and often enhance the value of the product (e.g. records and record players). Sellers may thus have some incentive to create standards, though they may be reluctant to relinquish a quasi-captive market and generally lower entry barriers. If there is competition in both markets, sellers may have a somewhat greater incentive and less ability to create standards. Once standards are established, however, these should prove quite stable since a single small competitor manufacturing only a part of the conjoint product can produce an incompatible line only at great risk. Here is a prime situation where standards, though currently useful, might deter some beneficial innovation. Where there is a dominant manufacturer in one line, his product usually becomes the pattern for informal standards, and for him, at least, the standard should prove but a small deterrent to change.

Firms often provide both parts of conjoint products. Where they also possess market power in one of these lines, it is likely that interchangeability standards will not emerge. For such firms frequently desire some sort of tying arrangement, which interchangeability standards help to destroy.

Tying

Tying is a business practice whereby a multiproduct firm typically conditions the sale/lease of one commodity (tying good), on the sale of another (tied good). Tying is involved in other business practices, such as full-line forcing. It is related to interchangeability standards, since lack of industrywide uniformities can implicitly tie products together, or help enforce an explicit tying arrangement. It is significant that antitrust cases dealing with tying often concern complementary products where interchangeability standards could exist: punch cards have been tied to computers,[4] repair parts to automobiles,[5] staples to stapling machines,[6] toilet paper to dispensers,[7] mimeograph supplies to mimeograph machines,[8] rivets to riveting machines,[9] etc.

Since firms that favor tying will generally oppose interchangeability standards, it seems worthwhile to examine some principal instances where tying appears a profitable practice. It should be noted, of course, that firms sometimes tie their products "defensively"—because others are tying theirs—and might actually prefer a situation without any tying at all, and with standards for interchangeability.

All tying depends on horizontal market power in the market for the tying good.[10] One common explanation for tying is the use of the tied good as a counting device to enhance monopoly profits via price discrimination. Many of the cases cited above are consistent with this hypothesis. If, rather than charge a uniform price, a monopolist can relate prices to intensity of demand, he can extract more of the consumers surplus and increase his profits. Effective price discrimination, however, requires determination of demand intensity and separation of markets. It may not be feasible for, say, a business machine monopolist to discriminate effectively by varying the price of only this single product. He may have great difficulty determining the present value of this durable good to customers, as well as preventing secondary sales from low-price to potential high-price buyers. A tying arrangement can remedy both these difficulties. Where direct metering is not practicable, a tied, overpriced, complementary product whose use reflects demand intensity may efficiently achieve the same result. Those using the machine more intensively end up, in effect, paying more for it.[11]

A related explanation for tying is to manipulate profits between the markets for the tying and the tied good. Assume that complements A and B are used together in varying proportions, with a monopolist producing item A and offering item B for sale in a competitive market. The monopolist might take the price of item B as given by competition, and then set the price for A. But because of the interrelation of demand curves, he may be able to increase total profits by tying, and raising the price of the tied good above the competitive level. This might be the case, say, if item B is used exclusively with A, demand for B is highly inelastic, and demand for A is not very responsive to B prices. The tying arrangement is profitable because the decrease in profits from the sale of A is more than compensated by the increase in profits from B.[12]

Tying should be viewed in this case as an attempt to raise the price of the tied product, and thus artificially restrict its supply. The higher price lowers the demand for the tying good, and hence its profit maximizing price. In certain circumstances it might be rational for the monopolist of A to lower price below cost, or possibly even give the item away.[13] The tying arrangements in this case need to be well policed, since competitors in B are willing to undersell the monopolist. (This is also true in the "counting device" example.) If we replace the monopolist in A with oligopolists, it is more easily seen how the lack of uniformity standards decreases policing problems. Without such standards the market for a particular type of B is more thin or separate, the number of direct competitors are fewer and enforcement costs should be less. Each oligopolist has fewer rival B producers to worry about.

A further related explanation for tying is simply to increase sales in an oligopolistic market. Assume some firms produce both A and B, and that in both markets price exceeds marginal cost. Say that buyers have definite preferences for A, but are relatively indifferent as to whose B product they buy. Then tying by any one firm may increase its sale of B, and its profits (though not total industry profits).[14] Producers benefiting most from tying will probably oppose possible uniformity standards. Indeed, for consumer products like razor blades or staples—though the above does not exactly describe such markets—lack of standards could well be the only tying arrangement.

The three related explanations for tying presented here clearly do not exhaust the possible profit-motives for tying. Other motives, for example, include evasion of price controls and the protection of goodwill. The examples are sufficient, though, for our purposes, to illustrate the close connection between tying and the lack of interchangeability standards. Instances when major firms would favor tying are often those where they will strongly oppose standardization.

On the other hand, Robert Kudrle, after examining the farm machinery industry, has argued that because of dynamic considerations, where there are other high entry barriers, major firms may at times actually prefer interchangeability standards as a hedge against risk. Since without compatability an important innovation by one company could swing demand to its *full* line, firms prefering the "quiet life" may favor interchangeability standards that would enhance security and stability of market shares. Kudrle found suggestive the fact that it was the policy of the farm machinery industry to freely license patented innovations.[15]

CONCLUDING COMMENTS

The principal benefit of voluntary industrywide interchangeability standards is that they widen markets, expanding alternative sources of supply. They can decrease search costs and entry barriers. Their effect on progressiveness is less clear. While increased competition might increase innovative activity, the standard itself may make radical design departures difficult. This seems more likely to be the case where the potential innovator does not produce both parts of the conjoint product.

    Market structure characteristics can strongly influence the incentive and ability to create interchangeability standards. A small number of large buyers can often coordinate their demand and effectively promote desired standardization. While sellers providing only one part of conjoint products may prefer interchangeability, those supplying both may have powerful incentives to oppose standards that help free quasi-captive markets. It should also be emphasized that even when interchangeability standards are widely desired, they need not automatically emerge, for there are change-over costs, bargaining problems, and the free-rider dilemma. The difficulties, as discussed in Chapter 1, of creating workable screw thread standards, or even track gauge standards, are indicative. Government might play a role in many of these areas where the free market is not creating socially beneficial standards.

    Interchangeability standards can clearly affect market structure and market conduct, by, for example, decreasing the possibilities for tying arrangements. On a wider scale, mention has been made of the potential influence of interchangeability standards on gift items, and on the profitability of theft. Their effect on the second hand business, and on repair industries should be even more pronounced.

    If we believe Alan Toffler,[16] the importance of standards for uniformity may decline in the future as technology makes it easier to create new varieties, and long production runs for *each* are not needed to attain lowest unit costs. If this is true, then solely from a *production*-economy viewpoint, uniformity standards will become less necessary. And if the future holds more rapid production changes, model changes, and trashing of products, real world benefits from interchangeability standards for replacement parts should also diminish.

    Since the topic was broad, these chapters on uniformity standards have not focused on many interesting questions, e.g., what exact standard is likely to be created (clearly technology is important) or when standards are easiest to enforce, or fashionable to break. Not much has been said about conversion costs, from the point of view of the firm or society. A careful distinction has not been made between standards that directly touch many industries (screw threads) and those that don't (railroad gauges). Nor have we distinguished interchangeability standards for parts of items bought in a lump (autos and parts) from tied components (guns and ammunition). These are some of the many areas that may deserve further thought and research.

Part III

Quality Standards

This Part deals with intercompany quality standards. These are universally minimum standards, and categorize products as either "better" (meeting the standard) or "worse" (not meeting it). Examples include the Boiler Code, ladder safety standards, gas appliance standards, paper cup quality standards, and the Comic Book Code of Ethics.

The principal function of voluntary quality standards is to supply information. Since the value of quality standards largely depends on the provision of useful information, and because the market for information is unusual, Chapter 6 is devoted to a discussion of the economics of information. The chapter is in some sense a digression from the main focus of the book, but appears necessary since the area is relatively new and unexplored. Three topics are discussed: (1) some general and singular characteristics of information as a commodity, (2) the possibility of asymmetry in product information between buyer and seller, and the potential for adulteration, and (3) various means by which the demand for product quality information is met. A major point of the analysis is that standards are but one of many alternative methods of providing quality information, with certain advantages and certain drawbacks.

Chapter 7 discusses grades, and analyzes the incentives to create intercompany quality standards, with particular emphasis on the relationship to market structure. A main purpose of that chapter is to provide clues concerning the proper place for governmental action.

Chapter Six

Product Quality Information

SOME SINGULAR CHARACTERISTICS
OF INFORMATION AS A COMMODITY

One of the assumptions for perfect competition is that decisionmakers have perfect information. This means, among other things, that gaining knowledge about prices and quality of products, as well as exchange opportunities, is costless, or that such information is a free good. In the real world, of course, information is usually a costly commodity, and economists have finally come to appreciate this enough to devote an appreciable amount of time and energy in an attempt to increase our knowledge about the economics of information. In the last few years there has been a flurry of academic articles dealing with the theory of information and, more specifically for our purposes, the "microeconomics of information"—the production, dissemination, and manipulation of information in a market context.[1]

As a commodity, information has some singular characteristics. First, information possesses many of the properties of a public good. Knowledge is a "non-rival good"; enjoyment of it by one individual does not decrease the amount available to others. Knowledge, in fact, is one of the few general things that can truly grow or evolve, as opposed to matter and energy, which are subject to the inexorable laws of conservation.[2] There are also usually economies of scale in the transmission of information; the extra cost of presenting a lecture or showing a TV program to an additional person is often close to zero. From an efficiency or welfare point of view, then, such information should be available virtually free of charge. But while this may lead to an optimal utilization of information, it provides little private incentive for the original collection or production of information.[3]

The producer of information, in some sense, has a monopoly, and he may seek to take advantage of this fact. An attempt to sell this information on the open market, however, may destroy the monopoly if others can reproduce the information at little cost to themselves. Even with elaborate and expensive security precautions, information often proves too intangible to be completely appropriable. Government measures to increase information production include patent laws, educational and research subsidies, etc.[4]

Independent producers of information on product quality (e.g., Consumers Union) face the inappropriability problem described above. Generally, governmental attitude in this area has been one of laissez-faire, combined with attempts to eliminate false advertising. Positive public action is largely limited to requiring some sellers to display certain information, such as food ingredients, gas octane ratings, and more recently car stopping distances and annual interest rates for loans.

Imperfect appropriability is only one of a number of factors leading to expected underinvestment in information production. Others include the riskiness of private research when combined with the lack of complete conditional-contract markets and the tendency for royalty schemes to not capture all benefits due to increasing returns in use.[5] On the other hand, there are considerations cutting in the opposite direction. If undiscovered ideas are like fish in the sea, subject to the rule of capture, and with patent rights going to the first in possession, then competitive invention is biased toward prematurity. Competition, combined with externalities, leads in this case to too many too small fish being caught.[6] The profit possibilities of "pushing"[7] information may increase information production. With respect to information on product quality, for example, high quality sellers may have an incentive not only to disseminate, but to create specific information about their particular product. Under a variety of assumptions, this can easily lead to overproduction of information. More on this later.

A second striking, and sometimes paradoxical, characteristic of information is that its value to a purchaser may be unknowable until the information has been purchased. Given incomplete appropriability, the seller cannot let the potential buyer carefully examine the information, for he then in effect may have acquired it without payment. This means that, from a welfare viewpoint, the potential purchaser must often base his buying decision on less than optimal criteria.[8] It means that there is often an incentive to devise schemes to demonstrate the content and accuracy of information without giving it away. And, as is the case for many products, sellers may wish to gain a reputation for producing or possessing a high quality item. This is true not only for a Consumers Union, but also for a research institute or management consulting group, or virtually any organization selling advice, analysis or information.

Any attempt to determine the authenticity of information or reliability of a source can encounter a theoretically endless process. Consider, for example, the case of a potential buyer of information. He is considering purchasing information from a particular source about expected product quality. In turn, an additional source of information on the reliability of this first source may be desired, and information may be wanted about the reliability of this second source, and so on without limit. In some theoretic sense, then, information on all relevant considerations can never be fully purchased on the market. Some must always come from one's own experience.[9] In some real sense, complete information is probably never available.

A further aspect of information, in this case information specifically about product quality, is that the costs of collecting or producing it for the products of an entire market is dependent, in part, on the structure of that market.[10] The more information that is required about more different products from more different producers, *ceteris paribus*, the more costly it is to collect. The more atomistic the market, the greater the product differentiation, the more product characteristics that are important, the more frequently they change, then the harder it will be to obtain reliable quality information about the entire market.

INFORMATION ASYMMETRY: THE
AKERLOF MODEL AND ADULTERATION

The brief description above seems to illustrate an important point, that information has some unusual characteristics, and that the market for information may be quite different from more familiar markets for, say, apples or desks. The market for product-quality information is obviously closely related to the market for the product in question; its demand can perhaps best be described as a derived demand. One of the most crucial elements of market structure (if not *the* most crucial element) is the availability of product and market information.

The literature not assuming perfect product information typically postulates that information endowments are asymmetrical. The seller knows more about the product quality than does the buyer. It is usually implicit that the seller knows at least as much about the market as does the buyer. This distinction between knowledge about the product and knowledge about the market seems important. The assumption that sellers know more about the product than buyers is generally a good one, though there are many minor exceptions (e.g., when I sell my car to the junkman, or my expert friend buys antiques). A similar *market* information assumption has less universality. The labor market serves as a counter-example, as does insurance (viewing the individual here as a seller of risk). An oft-made simplifying assumption of perfect seller knowledge is inappropriate for this book, since a major function of standards for uniformity is to provide market information to producers (e.g., Paper Stationery and Tablet Manufacturers Association's recommended sizes).

A second assumption of the typical model is that while buyers cannot determine the quality of a particular product (beforehand), they do know average market, or sub-market, quality. How they come by this information is not entirely clear, though one could postulate a number of plausible explanations. The assumption is not unreasonable for us since one motive for sellers to create industrywide quality standards is their belief that the shoddy products of a few firms reflect badly on the entire industry, that a few rotten apples spoil the barrel.

Akerlof shows that these assumptions cause "adverse selection."[11] Low quality sellers are encouraged to offer their products for sale; those with superior products are correspondingly discouraged. Bad products drive out the good. There is a reduction in the average quality level of goods (compared to a situation of perfect information), and also in the size of the market. In some cases the market may not be viable.

Put another way, there are externalities in the "averaging process" of buyers. The returns to a good quality item accrue to the entire industry rather than exclusively to the individual seller. Private and social returns differ and thus governmental action may increase social welfare.[12]

Akerlof examines markets where it makes little sense for the seller to reduce the quality level of the product (e.g., used car market, employment market). We might say he is focusing on sellers who are not producers. His model, though, is equally useful in explaining the incentive for producers to degrade product quality, assuming that costs are related to quality levels. To explain the dynamics of adulteration, however, slightly different postulates are needed. (With the Akerlof assumptions, and a smooth positive quality-cost relationship, then for producers/sellers, quality should immediately fall to zero, with all trade precluded.) Assume that buyers can tell whether or not quality falls within a certain small range around the perceived average, and that it takes time for buyers to notice any change in the average. Sellers then have an incentive to offer lower quality items within the range, and still lower quality once buyers realize the average has fallen. Such a simple model could explain the "salami tactics" of adulteration so prevalent in the real world.

What keeps quality from falling endlessly is often technological considerations. Alsberg describes the progressive deterioration of sole leather.[13] Over the years the leather became weighted more and more by tanning extract, glucose or Epsom salt. The limit for water soluble substances climbed continuously upward, until by 1931 a 33 per cent figure reflected "good commercial practice." "The figure cannot well go much higher," argued Alsberg, "because the tanner cannot get much more into the leather without risk of resulting trouble from spewing of the load." Chamberlin presents another example, the adulteration of mayonnaise.[14] The amount of gum arabic in mayonnaise rose quickly from 10 to 55 per cent. "If the producer had put any more gum arabic in the mayonnaise," argues Chamberlin, "it would probably have disintegrated." There are clearly factors other than technological considerations preventing unlimited product adulteration. Standards are one of these factors, e.g., doctor's standards of practice, lumber quality standards, and mandatory peanut butter standards.

The Akerlof model seems to assume that goods are "experience goods."[15] By this is meant that buyer evaluation of product quality can take place only after a purchase has been made. The quality of "inspection goods," on the other hand, can be determined before purchase. There is also an important third category of good in what actually is a continuum—those whose quality the buyer may never determine accurately (e.g., vitamins). These may be called "credence goods."[16]

Since quality is multidimensional, it is really for different aspects of the product that buyers judge quality by either "inspection," "experience," or "not at all." Product characteristics most susceptible to adulteration are those in the latter two categories. We should be surprised, therefore, if say hot dog appearance had declined through the years. (It hasn't.) On the other hand, we might anticipate that the meat content of franks could fall over time—which, indeed, it has.

MEETING THE DEMAND FOR
PRODUCT QUALITY INFORMATION

With a model permitting incomplete buyer information, ways of augmenting that information become important. Three methods will be briefly examined: unaided individual information gathering, contact with other users, and a potpourri category labeled "countervailing institutions," which includes advertising, guarantees, independent information producers, and standards.

If we consider only "inspection goods," with identical prices and the equivalent of only one aspect of quality about which there is complete agreement as to what is better or worse, then the individual search problem becomes identical to that described in the classic Stigler article.[17] Here, though, the buyer searches for quality given price, rather than vice versa. Quality dispersion now becomes a measure of the ignorance in the market. Rational buyers should continue to search as long as the expected utility is greater than the expected cost (which includes time without the product). We might expect a clustering of stores selling similar products, etc. Dropping any of the rigid assumptions, of course, makes the problem more realistic, and more difficult.

Now let full "experience goods" enter the model. We expect that experiments with (or sampling of) such goods will be more costly—the buyer has to purchase the product rather than inspect it. Thus, *ceteris paribus*, fewer experiments will be made for experience goods, allowing wider quality dispersion (given price), or increasing the price inelasticity of individual firms' demands curves. This is also the case for products purchased less often, for goods where quality change is frequent, etc.[18]

Another method of gaining product information is from the experience of other users, To the extent that contacts with other users are less frequent, or more difficult (e.g., because of geographical dispersion), information exchange will be less. Thus, as purchasers, we might expect stockbrokers to have better information than, say, farmers. This may be a rationale for government to help one group obtain information, but not the other.[19] Robert Nelson has developed a model in which the buyers decision rule is to purchase a particular brand only, and immediately, upon receiving an absolute number (e.g., 2) of personal testimonials as to its good quality.[20] The larger the original market share, and the smaller the rival firms, the progressively more likely is it for a particular brand to be the first to receive the needed testimonials. With this simple model, the only stable equilibrium is a monopoly.

Because product quality information is valued, and is not automatically available, devices arise and institutions emerge to provide it. These include advertising, brand names and guarantees, independent information producers, specifications, grades, and standards. The analysis of any of these, or others (e.g., "signalling"[21]) deserves at least a dissertation. For this book it seems enough to discuss very briefly a few of these, emphasizing that in the real world they are generally helpful—but not ideal—in providing information, and that they are often complements or substitutes for each other, each with its own comparative advantage. All, of course, can affect, and are affected by, market structure.

Advertising is the principal method by which individual firms "push" information about their specific products. There is clearly a tendency for such information to one-sided, and there is no surefire or cheap method to assess the bias. One doesn't need the theory of the Second Best (in this case, that "A little knowledge may be a dangerous thing") to realize that such information can sometimes have a detrimental effect on consumer decisions. The manner in which benefits and costs of advertising are related to market structure can also pose serious problems for society.

Individual sellers also have incentives to *create* positive information to "push." The laboratory documentations by one mouthwash manufacturer, for example, that his product "kills millions of germs on contact" may lead rational purchasers to switch brands. Similar findings by all manufacturers (with no actual change in the product) may leave buyers, in some sense, better informed, but no better off. From an efficiency point of view, too much information has probably been both created and disseminated.

On the other hand, sellers sometimes do not disseminate useful information seemingly detrimental to certain rivals. For example, if bleach is bleach, and aspirin aspirin, why wouldn't it pay a lower priced producer to point this out? In part, probably, because of fear of retaliation. In larger part because of external benefits. If A & P aspirin spent a lot of money—and it would take a lot—to convince the public that all aspirin is alike, then it would face a severe disadvantage in competition with Rix or Stop & Shop aspirin. And if all the independents got together to split the advertising cost, they would be making themselves vulnerable to new entrants.

Guarantees are another device by which information is disseminated. The guarantee (e.g., "triple your money back") may be viewed as a strategy by which the seller seems to alter his payoff matrix so that high quality (or truthfulness) appears as his rational course of action. Guarantees have limitations—being mainly applicable to experience attributes, and often facing high transactions costs as well as the potential "moral hazard" dilemma.

Consider the case of automobiles. The consumer has much better information about (information is cheaper to obtain about) certain aspects of performance (e.g., horsepower) than others (e.g., durability). Manufacturers thus have an incentive to provide good quality for the former aspects, and skimp on the latter. If guarantees are now introduced, and sellers bear the cost of lower durability, their incentives change for the better. There are problems, though, in that the determination of the cost of low durability is difficult or costly (e.g., how is time to be valued?). It may be costly to write and enforce rules (about road conditions, etc.), and a user can lose some of the incentive to take good care of his car, to treat it well. Thus many guarantees last only for a year—and much of the original problem remains.

Independent producers of information can furnish useful information on the quality of particular goods. There are a number of reasons, though, to expect that the amount of information supplied may be less than optimal. First there is the inappropriability problem discussed earlier. It is thus not surprising to learn that the secondary readership of *Consumer Reports* (magazine borrowers, library users, etc.) is as great as its original circulation. Consumer Union both collects and creates information. One type of information created may be its grading system, the assigning of weights to attributes allowing it to rank products. If CU did this excellently, it would face the appropriability problem. Presently, its problem is more one of creating and maintaining a reputation that, along with its sampling and testing, it does this reasonably well.

Another reason for the low sales and small amount of useful information provided by a Consumers Union is brand and variety proliferation, combined with rapid turnover in models (if not always in real quality). These factors make complete market information costly, as well as more rapidly obsolete.

A very important problem facing a Consumers Union is that, since a reputation for impartiality is essential, unlike most magazines it cannot generate revenues from advertisements. Since CU competes, in part, with these other magazines, it faces a comparative disadvantage. If CU could advertise while maintaining impartiality, each magazine it sells would generate more revenue (including advertising revenue). This would permit more funds to be spent for expanded facilities, improved testing, and generally better quality, which in turn would increase the number of magazines sold at any given price. Without ads, CU remains at a lower profit maximizing (or break-even) sales-quality position.

In the simple model below the firm tries to maximize profits (total revenue minus total cost).

$$\text{Maximize } TR\text{-}TC$$
$$\text{Let } TR = P_1 Q + P_2 Q$$
$$TC = L^* + P_3 Q$$
$$Q = f(P_1, L^*)$$

where P_1 = retail price
P_2 = advertising revenue/copy
P_3 = average cost of printing, etc.
L^* = amount spent on quality (number of tests, followups, etc.)
Q = Quality sold,

The argument is merely that as P_2 falls (to zero in the CU case) so generally will the profit-maximizing (Q,L^*) choice. Consumers receive less and poorer quality information than if CU could advertise and still be impartial.

While manufacturers use advertising to "push" positive information about their individual products, a Consumers Union has little incentive to push its market quality information (except perhaps as a loss-leader to demonstrate the worth of *Consumer Reports*). Thus final consumers must consciously *seek* such information (a process which has costs), as contrasted to being continuously innundated by advertising information via radio, TV, etc. In 1970 direct advertising reached the $21 billion level (excluding over $36 billion on personal selling costs). By contrast, all expenditures by consumer information organizations totaled only $13 *million*.[22]

A common method by which large buyers insure product quality information is by careful specification of desired quality. When General Motors wants a cleaner for a dirty painted wall, does it send a boy out to a grocery store? Not at all. It orders its "painted surface cleanser" by specification.[23] Specifications and brand names are substitutes for industrial buyers, and are used in varying degrees. Specifications are often preferable because they invite competitive bidding. Less reliance needs to be placed on the integrity of an individual seller, and the risk is less that quality will change with subsequent purchases.[24] By making things specific, the specification eliminates much of the fuzziness in exchange. A buyer receiving an inferior product can frequently claim breach of contract, rather than merely registering a complaint. However, when it is costly to write specifications (actually, it is sometimes impossible to write specifications—e.g., to cover intangible quality aspects such as "workmanship") purchase description is often made by brand name.[25]

Specifications generally make sense only for large purchases of a single commodity. For a small buyer, such as a consumer, the original cost of specification—learning what aspects are crucial, writing the specification, and perhaps even testing the product—proves too enormous. In the real world, this high fixed cost of specification means, in effect, that there are economies of scale in buying. The large purchaser gets better information and thus a better product for his money. This important conclusion is true not only for specifications, but under most information collection assumptions.

Quality Standards

Standard specifications, what this book calls standards, provide a related method for securing product quality information. Standard specifications are merely particular specifications used by a number of different buyers. Generally they are formal standards, created for the particular purpose of becoming industrywide standards, and written by representatives from a variety of firms and institutions.

When available, standard specifications have some definite advantages for buyers. Since they are generally created by the consensus of diverse and knowledgable parties, they should be reasonably good. They can thus be used with some security. The buyer is saved the expense of writing his own specification, and of gaining knowledge about all the relevant aspects of quality. These have been reduced to one: The product does or does not meet the standard. Most importantly, like standards for uniformity, standard specifications serve a coordinating function, providing a focal point for purchase. The very fact that others purchase by standards can benefit the buyer qua buyer. For one thing, as standards become widely known, this should reduce the negotiation burden and decrease misunderstandings and disputes.[26] Additionally, by ordering by standards the purchaser promotes price competition, since sellers are already producing such varieties. Conversely, it takes time, and risk, to quote on unusual specifications and fewer sellers are willing to complete for the order. Buying by standards also allows potential scale production economies, permits quick delivery, and insures future availability. All these factors effectively lower price. Furthermore, because standard items have been purchased by a large number and variety of users, information about them is great, and can be obtained through observation, personal contacts, trade journals, etc.[27]

On the other hand, standards may be more costly to write than specifications, since they require some consensus. Or they may be expensive to purchase from a standards writing organization. Since they are employed for different purposes, standard specifications can sometimes be too general, or not perfectly suitable for a particular use. Additionally, technological change can decrease the value of a standard. The buyer often needs information on the current "quality" of the standard itself before he confidently can use it for making purchases.

CONCLUDING COMMENTS

The economics of information is an important and fascinating topic about which much should, but not much has, been written. This chapter contained, in part, a quick review of the literature dealing with product quality information. It emphasized that information is an unusual commodity, possessing some singular characteristics. The Akerlof model of asymmetrical information and averaging externalities was examined in relation to adulteration. The prevention of adulteration is discussed in Chapter 7 as one of the incentives favoring the creation of industrywide standards. Finally, various methods of providing product information were analyzed; none of them proved totally adequate. Purchasing by standard specifications is one possible method, with its own peculiar advantages and drawbacks.

The major beneficial property of quality standards is that they serve to coordinate purchases, providing a focal point for demand. It clearly makes a tremendous difference what exactly the standard says, where actually the focal point is. Chapter 8 examines the important and intimately related question "Who really writes standards?" Unfortunately, many socially useful standards are never created, while some detrimental standards are. So Chapter 7 deals with the incentive and ability to write standards, particularly in relation to market structure. Further discussion of standards as information is presented there.

Chapter Seven

Quality Standards and Market Structure

TYPES OF QUALITY STANDARDS

This book includes a variety of standards under the heading of quality standards, to be differentiated from the often dimensional standards for uniformity. Upon examining these quality standards, at least three ideal types tend to emerge— terminology and measurement standards, minimum standards, and standard test procedures. The distinction between these types is sometimes blurred, and it is not unusual for a single standard specification to contain elements of all three.

Many, in some sense most, standards are merely definitions, or more accurately, agreements on definitions.[1] Industrywide terminology and measurement standards are clearly of this type. Formal nomenclature standards are most useful when general language or convention may prove unclear or imprecise. To avoid confusion or misunderstanding, standard specifications usually include technocal definitions of the terminology employed. Thus Aluminum Standards and Data,[2] a 1972 publication of the Aluminum Association, has sixteen pages of standard nomenclature, defining general terms from "annealing" to "yield strength." The association has also developed a uniform numbering system for designating wrought aluminum and wrought aluminum alloys, as well as the tempers in which aluminum, aluminum alloy wrought products, and aluminum alloy castings are produced.[3] The fundamental purpose of such standards is clearly to facilitate and simplify communication.

The absence of understandable terminology standards, especially for consumer items, can cause much confusion. The National Industrial Conference Board,[4] for example, questioned: "Does solid mahogany mean all mahogany, or a solid table with a mahogany finish?" "What is raw silk; a part-wool blanket; oak tanned leather?" With widely used terminology standards, consumer information could certainly be enhanced; the standards would help eliminate much of the fuzziness in exchange.

Like standards of terminology, industrywide measurement standards are primarily definitions. They represent agreement on how best to measure certain aspects of the product in question. They are economically useful in that they decrease negotiation costs, facilitate product comparison, and lessen the possibility of misunderstanding. Common examples of such standards include methods for measuring various characteristics of tuners and amplifiers,[5] for determining refrigerator capacities,[6] and even for measuring office floor space.[7]

An accepted method of measurement, especially concerning product aspects where better or worse is at issue, (as opposed to dress size measurement standards, or those for shoe lasts),[8] can significantly affect incentives. To use a minor example, the measurement standards for refrigerator capacity is widely employed throughout the industry, with manufacturers often certifying their claims. Yet Consumers Union argues that the standard is a poor one, taking no consideration of space-consuming items such as shelves, trays, light shields, trim or unhandy space. The manufacturers, CU claims, should be given an incentive not just to provide more space in refrigerators, but more usable space.[9]

Agreement not only concerning how to measure an aspect of performance, but what aspects should be measured, can fundamentally affect incentives. And the creation of formal measurement standards usually indicates a collective decision that those quality characteristics are important enough to measure. Sometimes such an industrywide agreement is reached from discussion of those quality claims that require certification. For example, in the 1950s room air conditioner performance was advertised in a variety of ways: in terms of horsepower, watts, tons, room-size cooled, etc. As is the case with many products, it was difficult for consumers to make intelligent comparisons. Additionally, manufacturers' claims were often of doubtful validity. It seemed that these problems could be discouraging consumers from trying the new product. It was also known that the Federal Trade Commission had started an investigation. In response, the industry, through its trade association, created a certification program. Furthermore, after lengthly discussion, it was agreed that there were three crucial performance measures for room air conditioners: watts, amps, and BTUs. The industry certification program emphasizes these three performance characteristics, and it is upon these three that product competition now focuses.[10]

Closely associated with measurement standards are standard test methods. Such formal industrywide standards can prove useful where no single procedure stands out as the best way to test a product characteristic. A principal benefit, then, of standard test methods, like standard specifications, is that they help provide uniformity. When it is known, for example, that steel coming from different producers, or even different countries, has been tested by identical procedures, the respective test results can be quickly understood and confidently compared by potential steel purchasers.

Many trade associations and engineering societies prepare standards for testing product characteristics. The Perlite Institute, for example, publishes

"Test Methods and Related Standards," which contains standard procedures for evaluating the quality of expanded perlite.[11] The Northern Textile Association has developed test methods to determine original elongation, original tension, and loss of tension under heat for the woven elastic in male underwear.[12] When it became evident that wide deviations in test results were being obtained from different laboratories for different products, the Air Diffusion Council decided to establish a common method for testing air diffusion equipment. Its thirty-three-page Equipment Test Code helps standardize testing procedures.[13] Major benefits from such a code are improved information and decreased costs. The manufacturers themselves, for example, no longer have to make up "test mock ups" to evaluate performance data. The availability of better data to architects and engineers, the council argues, should contribute to a better design of systems.[14]

The type of quality standards focused upon in this chapter are minimum standards, industrywide agreements that generally draw a line indicating that certain products are "better" (they meet the standard), while others are "worse" (they don't meet the standard). Examples include standard specifications for paints,[15] plastic material,[16] and rubber products.[17] A minimum quality standard has been promulgated for shoe laces. This specified, for example, that yarn should be of at least 30/2 KPM cotton, there should be 44 ends of yarn, at least 28 picks per inch, and the tips must be a minimum of 17/32 inches long.[18]

It remains to mention a number of items, not emphasized in this book, that are often considered as standards, or in connection with standards. "Use recommendations" represent one such group. The National Lime Association, for example, has created recommendations to assist lime consumers in the most efficient utilization of quick and hydrated lime.[19] Such suggestions to buyers are probably not "product standards," but their purpose is evident—to help increase the value of the product to the purchaser. "Recommended Practices" that relate to the manufacture of the product are categorizable as parts of minimum quality standards.

Standards for services, such as those for the training of lifeguards and diving judges,[20] or the qualifications examination of welders,[21] are considered outside the scope of this study.

Certification and labeling are often discussed in connection with quality standards. *Standards* for certification, however, are usually testing standards or perhaps standards for the testing agencies themselves. Standards for labels are usually uniformity standards (for easy reading) and/or minimum standards (for informational content).

GRADES

Classification and grading are often mentioned in conjunction with standards. Classification generally refers to the dividing of a commodity into lots which have uniform characteristics, without intending either superior or inferior groupings. Often within classifications, grading is performed. This is more than a simple further separation; for better or worse is now at issue. Grades are a rank ordering of products, using minimum standards as the dividing lines.

As might be expected, graded commodities generally lack strong brand identification. Grades give buyers a summary appraisal of product quality, providing the same summary appraisal for all purchasers. Grades thus tend to make buyers better informed, and lead them to rank products similarly. Grading thereby eliminates some product differentiation advantages, making established sellers' demand curves more elastic, and generally lowering entry barriers.

Grades make certain quality information available to all. If the government, for example, sets grades and tests products, some of the scale economies in purchasing—economies due to the costs of obtaining product quality information—are eliminated. As with independently written standard specifications, the big purchaser might lose some of his advantages over the small. From the seller standpoint, grades eliminate much of the potential scale advantages in quality assurance.

Over some range, the average cost of assuring quality declines as direct assurance expenditures (e.g., advertising the results of tests performed at the firm's request by independent laboratories) increase. Perhaps more important, the average cost of assuring quality also declines for the firm as quantity sold increases. When a particular brand has high (present and past) sales, a potential purchaser finds it easier to obtain "testimonials" from other users,[22] and is more likely himself to have had experience with that brand. A large established multiproduct company thus has the greatest potential quality assurance advantages. This is true even for entirely new product lines, for quality is now "guaranteed" by a firm whose reputation is wellknown.

The fact that grades decrease differentiation advantages is a crucial and often overlooked point. Grades generally permit the small seller to compete more effectively with the large. One effect of meat grading, for example, may be to decrease seller concentration in the market.

Grades help firms lacking differentiation advantages, and generally tend to decrease the value of built-up reputation and trade names. Firms possessing certain product differentiation advantages tend, therefore, to resist attempts to initiate a grading system. It is not surprising that major paper companies and automobile tire manufacturers, for example, have long opposed grades for their products.

Commodities actually graded in the United States include milk, eggs, wool, lumber, mushroom, soybeans, meat, scrap iron, and diamonds. As theorized, major brand names are generally not important in such markets, and small firms face little product differentiation disadvantages. Additionally, graded commodities are often those for which existing firms might have had difficulty establishing quality assurance—product differentiation advantages, and therefore where resistance to grading was probably least. A usual feature of product currently graded, for example, is that their quality does not predominantly depend on "factory control" procedures, but on more unpredictable factors, often on nature. The number of knots in a given piece of lumber, for instance, is somewhat of a stochastic variable, and largely independent of the ability or efficiency of the "manufacturer."

Currently graded commodities seem to be those which were most susceptible to grading; from a slightly different perspective, it can be argued that they were the most desirable candidates *for* grading. When goods are produced by many and scattered firms grading can provide the greatest assistance to buyers, for as was explained in Chapter 6, a large number of geographically disperse sellers can make search costs high. Grades should be the most help to purchasers when other substitutes, such as brand names, do not exist. And the fact that products currently graded are often primary goods makes them more amenable to grading. The primary nature of these commodities usually means it is easier to discover some generally agreed-upon quality rank-ordering, and their "God-made" property lessens the potential problem that grades might inhibit major design breakthroughs.

Firms with product differentiation advantages will usually oppose grades. They generally argue that their products are not suitable for grading. Among other things, they claim that the goods possess many non-collinear but highly important product quality characteristics. Absorptiveness, softness, and strength, for example, are important aspects of paper towels, and it may depend on use or preference whether an absorptive weak towel is considered superior to a strong but less absorptive one.[23] Consumers, of course, could benefit in this case if *each* of the product attributes were graded, or if complete grades were given by product *use*. Manufacturers also argue that grades may focus competition on the wrong areas. For example, certain characteristics of writing paper, such as appearance, formation, printability, and lack of curl, presently defy accurate measurement. "If," claim producers, "the setting of definite standards for the measurable characteristics is carried to extremes, this would tend to limit manufacturers in developing some of the unmeasurable characteristics that are often far more important in the market place."[24] The implication is generally that buyers won't understand the information provided, and will buy blindly by grade—and that their resulting purchases will be "worse" than had they received no grade information at all.

While strong brand differentiation may sometimes be preferable to grading, it seems that, if properly understood, grades can provide succinct and useful product information for a wide variety of commodities. Standard grading systems can decrease explanation and confusion costs, increase comparability, as well as neatly packaging information. Commodities currently graded seem ideal for grading, and it is difficult to discover cases where the grading should be stopped. On the other hand, inadequate buyer knowledge and power plus individual seller unwillingness to relinquish brand advantages seem often to combine to prevent the creation of other beneficial grading systems. The next section of this chapter deals with the incentive and ability to create minimum standards.

INCENTIVE TO CREATE MINIMUM STANDARDS

The major informational benefits from quality standards, particularly standard specifications, have already been discussed. The benefits are due largely to the coordination function performed by standards, and accrue primarily to buyers. It seems plausible, then, to argue that the main impetus for standardization comes from buyers, and an examination of a wide number and variety of existing standards appears to substantiate this hypothesis. A problem arises, however, in that purchasers, especially final consumers, are often too atomistic and disorganized to push for standards effectively. Thus with respect to final goods, voluntary standardization is rare, quality standards arising mainly in areas where their existence benefits producers or sellers. (Where minimum standards are primarily to permit functional interchangeability between parts or products, the analysis in Chapter 5 applies.)

In the discussion that follows, attention is first focused on the incentives and ability of buyers to create minimum standards; then the seller side of the market is examined. While other specific interest groups may prove the prime movers for standardization (e.g., the National Society for the Prevention of Blindness promulgates eye safety standards),[25] this is a rare occurrence, the large majority of standards being the result of direct pressure from buyers, sellers, or both. The role played by the government in quality standardization is mentioned briefly, and examined in depth in Chapter 8.

It is sometimes argued that many important standards were created to solve particular social problems, with buyer and seller interests only part of the larger public interest. Such cases, however, generally represent instances where buyers or sellers have forced standardization, or more usually, they are fundamentally in agreement that standards will prove helpful. The Boiler Code may serve as an example. The problem, recognized as such by everyone, was that boilers often, and spectacularly, exploded, causing loss of life and property damage. In 1914, relying on a great deal of scientific research on the characteristics of metals under high temperatures, the American Society of Mechanical Engineers produced its famous Boiler Code. Continually revised and presently containing over 1,000 pages, the Code is generally followed, is mandatory in many states, and has been instrumental in dramatically reducing the hazards associated with boilers.[26]

There are some instances where the government has created voluntary standards. (A point to be emphasized is that there are few other groups around neither representing nor dominated by buyers or sellers that write standards.) The electrical safety code, for example, was originally written by the National Bureau of Standards over the protests of the industry, which claimed it infringed on managerial perogatives and gave undue publicity to the hazards of electricity. Though available, in its early days the code was not widely used save in those few states which adopted it as law.[27]

Buyers

Buyers generally have less information about the product than do sellers. Sellers, who are sometimes the producers, usually have had the good in their immediate possession, and, perhaps, are more likely to specialize in handling the item. It is thus the buyer who usually wants to know more information about the product. Standard specifications provide one means by which buyers can obtain such information. Whether or not these standards exist often depends on whether or not buyers can convert their desires into an effective demand. Large or organized purchasers generally can. Small, disorganized ones cannot. The argument is that a crucial factor determining the usefulness and existence of voluntary industrywide standards in various markets is the number of buyers and size of their purchases.

Over twenty years ago, and on much the same issue, Scitovsky emphasized the importance of the buyers' side of the market.[28] The grading or standardization of products, he argued, should not be considered data, as Marshall assumed. Instead they depend on the expertness of the buyer. The expert buyer insists on comparing rival products, and this insistence forces sellers, or makes it profitable for them, to make their products easily comparable. Thus Scitovsky argues, expertness of buyers leads to standardization.

Scitovsky's "expertness" argument is similar but not identical to that presented in this book. Here the crucial variables are the more easily determined: size of purchases, and number of buyers. Purchase size seems a reasonable and simply proxy for the absolute monetary importance of product information to a buyer. Large buyers should generally be more expert, because it pays to be. Standards are one way they increase their information. Number of buyers is included as one influential factor determining the ease with which buyers can coordinate their purchases.

Drawing heavily on the Scitovsky article, a recent Federal Trade Commission study reaches conclusions similar to his. The preliminary report of the FTC Task Force on Industry Self-Regulation asserts: "It is the character of the market on the buying side . . . that largely determines the kind of quality of the standardization-certification program a given industry will be expected to develop."[29] These range from the well-informed market at one extreme (e.g., the market for raw steel) to the uniformed market at the other (e.g., the market for analgesics).

A further testimonial to this proposition is given by a high official of a leading standardizing society. He writes:

> The strongest impetus for the development of a particular standard is that exercised by users who demand solution to some problem which has vexed them in the market place. Users who are organized in their own industry organization have become most powerful in this respect and through threats of writing their own standard, frequently push manufacturers into efforts they might not otherwise undertake . . .
>
> It is an obvious axiom that manufacturers are exceedingly reluctant to relinquish any flexibility that they might exercise in the production of their products. By contrast, users are most strenuous in their demands for the maximum degree of standardization to eliminate work for themselves.[30]

A principal piece of evidence supporting the contention that buyers are usually the motivating force behind standardization is the fact that most available standards are for producers' goods. Comparatively, there are few useful voluntary standards for final goods. Recently, for example, the National Commission on Product Safety examined the forty-four categories of consumer products which cause the highest number of estimated annual injuries in the home. These products include swings, toys, bottles, bicycles, glass doors, and power drills. Twenty-six of these product categories were not covered by any voluntary industrywide safety standard. A careful evaluation of seven of the remaining eighteen products failed to turn up standards for even one that were considered close to being adequate. For instance, on the standard for rotary lawn mowers, the commission argued that there was a need for requiring such inexpensive items as a disconnect between the power drive and cutting blade; an anti-roll back device for mowers not self-propelled; location of the "pull" starting mechanism only on the side opposite the starting chute; leakproof and childproof gas caps, etc.[31]

Unlike the large corporate buyer, the small, inexpert, unorganized consumer generally has no way of effectuating his desire for standards, save through the political process. Indeed, the rise of consumerism in the late 1960s, leading to a wave of mandatory standardization (e.g., National Traffic and Motor Vehicle Safety Act, the National Gas Pipeline Safety Act, the Fair Labelling and Packaging Act, etc.) has had a noticeable impact on voluntary standardization and standardizing societies. In the late 1960s standards spokesmen began emphasizing the need for final goods standards. For example American Society for Testing and Materials (ASTM) president F. J. Mardulier, in a speech entitled "Is There a Future for Voluntary Standardization?", argued that the demand for consumer standards would eventually be met. "The question is," he said, will it be met voluntarily by industry, or will government find it necessary to step in and fill the vacuum formed by industry's inaction?

Until now, most of the standards produced by ASTM have been industrial standards, that is both the producer and consumer of the product being standardized are industries. The 4000 standards produced by ASTM over the past 70 years are recognized throughout the world as competent, authoritative and indispensable to the rational exchange of industrial materials . . .

The question remains: can ASTM write a similar record in the field of consumer standards?[32]

A. Q. Mowbray, a writer on consumer affairs, reported a stirring within the industry:

A large and growing number of responsible manufacturers—no doubt motivated in part at least by the "threat" of governmental action—are attempting to persuade industry leaders that the voluntary system, which has worked so well in providing the thousands of standards by which industrial products are bought and sold, must be brought to bear on the vast unsolved problem of standards for consumer products.[33]

Government action in certain areas, by increasing the threat of action in others, clearly had spill-over effects. Standardizing organizations made more of a show "beating the bushes" for consumer or public interest representatives to serve on the various committees. The central clearinghouse for voluntary standards, USASI, boasted rather presumptuously in 1966: "The waif of voluntary national standardization—the individual consumer—now has a permenant home. He has been adopted by the United States of America Standards Institute."[34] Investigations such as those by the National Commission on Product Safety produced a flurry of standardizing activities in related areas. But while many organizations began to consider consumer standards more seriously, the overwhelming focus of the voluntary system remained on producers' goods.

The dearth of useful voluntary standards for consumer goods is consistent with the hypothesis that buyer power is usually a prerequisite for their creation. While no formal survey concerning the impetus for standardization has ever been attempted, it does seem, upon some examination, that effective buyer demand is generally crucial. The SAE-standard steel case, discussed at length in Chapter 2, serves as a good illustration of buyers imposing standards upon recalcitrant sellers. A similar example concerns the SAE and oil refineries. In the twenties, after much research and experimentation, the SAE created a system for the determination of motor oil viscosity, a system of far greater precision and accuracy than the then current arbitrary seller designation of "light," "medium," or "heavy." While some refineries worked with the society to help formulate the standards, others opposed any labeling of their cans or barrels with such ratings as decreasing the value of their built-up reputation, "detracting from the individuality of the brand."[35]

Actually, the auto firms wrote these standards not principally as purchasers of motor oil, but as makers of a complementary product. Better consumer information about the proper oil to use adds to the worth of car ownership. The National Petroleum News recognized this fact, editorializing in 1928

> High speed cars are expensive and their buyers are mostly men who expect perfect performance for their investment and who kick strenuously if they do not get it. The automobile manufacturers cannot afford to displease such customers, so they specify carefully the oil that is likely to give most satisfactory service in high-speed, expensive cars. This was the main reason for the formulation of the SAE specifications by the automobile engineers.[36]

The role of complementary industries in creating standards is discussed further in the subsequent section.

Now the petroleum industry itself writes standards through its trade association, the American Petroleum Institute, but these standards concern products purchased by the industry (e.g., specifications for steel plug valves with flanged ends, or recommended practices for electrical installations in petroleum refineries).[37] The API says,

> All of our standards are written from the point of view of a consuming industry ... Our motive simply is to provide uniform performance requirements to the widest possible range of suppliers, while maintaining the level of operational efficiency, safety and durability suited to the needs of any and all companies engaged in petroleum operations.[38]

The argument thus far has been that buyers mainly benefit from minimum standards, and that with large buyers, especially from within the same industry, the needed coordination for effective standardization is more easily achieved. An examination of the real world has tended to support the conclusion that without powerful and expert buyers most standard specifications would probably never be written.

The argument, however, would be incomplete without a discussion of the distribution of benefits among buyers. For on first glance it appears that while the gains from industrywide standards may be absolutely greater for large purchasers (they buy more) than for small, the benefits may be *relatively* less since large firms begin with scale advantages in writing their own company specifications. Initially, then, it might seem that large buyers would refuse to participate in the creation of standards that could lessen their competitive advantage. This indeed is a major explanation for the non-involvement of the giants in the early auto parts standardization by the SAE.

There are strong counter-arguments to this line of analysis. First is the problem of appropriability. One institution's specifications may be used by others, as for example, government purchase specifications are widely used throughout industry, and vice versa.[39] Thus the relative gains to small firms from standard specifications may not be so great—they may previously have had the alternative of "stealing" the individual specifications of large rivals. In other words, the real economies of scale in purchasing may not be as large as assumed. But suitability, of course, must be taken into consideration. Specifications should be most suited for the buyers that write them. The same, though, is true for standards. It thus may make sense for large firms to push for standards, especially those standards most suitable for themselves.

In the real world, big companies may consider standardization from their own immediate narrow perspective, rather than being concerned with possible effects on small competitors. Moreover, large firms may not view small companies as important rivals. By having a central industrywide organization write the (standard) specifications, creation costs are decreased for the firm, and information is gained not only from the give and take of standardization meetings, but also, eventually, from others experience in using the identically specified product. The resulting cost reductions may represent important immediate goals for organizational decisionmakers. Profits and sales can rise, even if costs for all firms in the market are similarly cut (oligopoly). This is especially true when there is strong interindustry competition (industry demand is very elastic).

Presently, most voluntary standards-making organizations are dominated by large firms. This is generally the case for both the trade associations and engineering societies that write most of the formal standards in the United States. It is not difficult to understand why small business is often underrepresented in the standardization process. The problem is that the absolute cost in terms of time and money of sending an employee representative to meetings is the same for the small as for the big business. But less of the total benefit of standards is internalized for the small firm. Moreover, without coordinated action, any individual small concern may correctly feel that, singly, it will be unable to substantially alter the resulting standard. Another problem limiting small firm participation is that since the matters covered at meetings are often highly technical and esoteric, it may not be readily known whether a small company has an expert in the particular field.[40]

The domination of big business over the standardization process is further enhanced by the fact that many standards committees have little money for research. If needed research on a question is to be performed, business, particularly big business, must be convinced that it is in its own interest to underwrite the cost.[41] Via its resources and research facilities, the large-scale enterprise may fundamentally determine the content of standards, as well as what standards get written. It is thus not surprising to find that many smaller companies are quite suspicious of voluntary standardization.[42] (For more on this topic, see Chapter 8.)

Sellers

The principal impetus for standardization usually comes from buyers. Established sellers, on the other hand, often want to preserve product differentiation advantages, and thus oppose the creation of minimum standards. Without sufficient buyer pressure to counter these strong vested interests, generally little industrywide standardization will occur. As the National Industrial Conference Board (NICB) concluded in its 1929 survey of standards:

> Wherever extensively exploited trade or brand names or patent rights are involved, standardization has made little headway. The object of trade and brand names is to build up good-will and lift goods out of competition. The object of standards and specifications is primarily to eliminate superficial differences and to center attention on price. Manufacturers do not want to sacrifice a trade advantage based upon good-will secured through the popularization of a trade or brand name by admitting that their product is made according to a specification followed by the entire trade.[43]

While small concerns or potential entrants might gain from the information that standards provide to buyers, without strong buyer support their power is rarely enough to create effective standards. Even if most sellers are indifferent rather than opposed to standardization, there is little reason to expect that minimum industrywide standards will somehow spontaneously arise. The "natural" order of things is usually for there to be no standards, for creation often takes time, energy, expense, and cooperation.

There are, of course, occasions when most sellers actually favor standardization. (Standards for consumer goods are far from unknown.) It is the purpose of this section to examine some of the most important instances when sellers have the incentive, and the ability, to create industrywide minimum quality standards.

Expected Governmental Action. A prime motive for sellers to produce their own minimum standards is to thwart anticipated government interference. A classic example concerns the Code of the Comics Magazine Association of America. The effect of mass media upon juvenile delinquency was a major public issue in 1954. The voluntary comics code, adhered to by more than 85 per cent of the comic book publishers, was adopted in that year as the basis for the industry's program of self-regulation. The industry was assuring parents and legislators that its house was now in order—it guaranteed that high standards of decency and morality would be followed by those large majority of comics bearing the Code Seal of Approval.[44]

The code, enforced by an independent authority, forbids profanity, vulgarity, nudity, rape, excessive depravity, sadism, etc. Crimes are never to be presented in a way to promote distrust of the forces of law or justice, or inspire readers with a desire to imitate criminals. Divorce is never to be treated humorously or represented as desirable, etc.[45]

Whether consumers recognize the seal and buy by it may not be crucial. The important consideration seems to be that the code represents an agreement among sellers on what constitutes above and below standard, and demonstrates to government that the vast majority of comics manufacturers are capable of regulating themselves.

The increased governmental concern with consumer protection in recent years has prompted expanded industrywide efforts at self-regulation. The white goods industry may serve as an illustration. The Association of Home Appliance Manufacturers is a strong, professional, and progressive trade association. It not only serves its membership, but has often taken a leadership position; and one place where AHAM has displayed its leadership is in the area of standards development. Interacting more with governmental and consumer groups than do its member companies, AHAM has generally been quicker to see the need and promise of both safety and measurement standards, and has been instrumental in their creation. As Herb Phillips, Technical Director of AHAM, stated:

> In today's society, any industry as conspicuous as the major home appliance industry is continually faced with the threat of governmental regulation. The only way to avoid governmental regulation is to more faster than the government. The alternative to governmental regulation, in my opinion, is judicious self-regulation. AHAM will play an increasingly active role in this area.[46]

Many of AHAM's staff felt that to provide leadership in this area while maintaining the satisfaction of the member companies would be the key challenge of the 1970s.[47]

It might be hypothesized that industries most threatened by possible governmental consumer protection regulation would be conspicuous ones, like the home appliance industry, perhaps with conspicuous firms, like General Electric. But how to operationally define "conspicuousness" in order to test the hypothesis could prove a definite problem.

Voluntary standardization efforts may make sense even when mandatory standards are expected. This is because the existence of a voluntary standard can significantly affect the subsequent government regulations. The issues involved in standardization are often so technical that government may not have the in-house experts necessary to independently determine an appropriate standard. Since the writing of a good standard entails some cost, government is likely to be receptive to any existing consensus standard, especially when written by a broad spectrum of interests to whom the government itself might reasonably turn for technical assistance. Many government standards were thus originally voluntary standards, accepted as mandatory without substantial modifications. This is probably the case for most building codes, as well as for aviation, automotive, and labor safety standards. The industry, if its consensus standard is accepted as law, can be assured that the standard is technically sound, not generally detrimental to the entire industry, and perhaps especially beneficial to those who dominated the creation process.

Adulteration, Averaging, and Differentiated Products. Begin with the Akerlof assumption, that buyers can tell average product quality within an industry, but not the quality of a particular item. Let this also mean that any individual seller would find it too costly to distinguish his product, even if he wanted to. Sellers may, for example, be too small and potential customers too scattered for major attempts at product differentiation to prove profitable. Let industry demand depend principally on price and average product quality. And finally assume that from the industry's viewpoint, average product quality is below optimal. Numerous buyers desiring high quality items may be looking elsewhere.

Unfortunately, if acting individually, sellers have little incentive to upgrade their products, since any benefits accrue to the industry as a whole. Indeed, the individual incentives of any seller may be to decrease quality and cut costs. As a group, however, they have a strong desire to raise average quality, and thus a powerful motive to create minimum industrywide product standards.

An excellent case study is provided by the experience of Japanese export industries in the postwar period. Before World War II, cheap Japanese goods had flooded world markets, but were generally known for their low quality. After the war, Japan decided that it must alter that reputation if its goods were to compete in the expanding markets for high quality items. While an individual manufacturer might have little incentive to upgrade his product, collectively the incentive was strong.[48]

In 1949 the Japanese government, with manufacturers' blessings, enacted its comprehensive exports standards and inspection law, perhaps the first of its kind in the world. Some 40 per cent of all Japanese exports are covered by this law. Manufacturers whose goods have passed the many detailed quality standards are licensed to afix the JIS (Japanese Industrial Standard) seal of approval on their products. Part of the rapid increase in Japanese exports is generally credited to this guarantee of product quality.[49]

Significantly, most products bearing the JIS mark are produced by small- or medium-sized firms.[50] These are the firms expected to have the most difficulty in distinguishing their products. By acting collectively, in this case under governmental auspices, these companies seem to be able to achieve the scale economies in guaranteeing product quality that is already possessed by the large scale enterprise. And *national* standards probably make good sense for Japanese exports since "averaging" externalities may also occur between industries (e.g., one bad Japanese product may make Americans leery of buying completely different Japanese products). To be effective the JIS seal must provide information to buyers, or the standard must be enforced. Otherwise, manufacturers again have an incentive to adulterate.

A primary function of minimum standards can be to guarantee product quality. The industrywide standard may reduce the risk of purchase, or cost of search, and thereby increase total sales (and at least short-run profits). An industry composed of sellers lacking major product differentiation advantages may therefore have a strong incentive to create quality standards, especially if adulteration is likely and close product substitutes are available. Strong interindustry competition, when combined with the other market characteristics mentioned, can thus promote trade association sponsored standardization.

The 1929 survey of standardization by the NICB, for example, disclosed a large number of instances where increased interindustry competition had intensified standardization activities. The zinc industry, by the establishment of standards (and by advertising), was attempting to win back the metal roofing market, lost largely to tin and cooper sheeting producers. The decline in the popularity of galvanized iron had been "partly due to the entire lack of quality standards among certain producers in the industry in the past."[51] Brick manufacturers were taking up standardization "on a larger scale than heretofore as a method of combatting the competition of the cement industry."[52] The tile and marble industries were turning to industrywide standards as a partial solution to the difficulties of competition with newer types of floor surfacing materials (linoleum, abrasive compositions, etc.)[53] Interindustry competition played an important role in the creation of quality standards for gas appliances. The gas industry, containing over 240 manufacturers of gas ranges and 140 space heater producers, had used standardization for some time to help meet strenuous competition from oil, wood, coal, and electricity. By 1927 gas ranges had to pass more than 160 tests in order to be certified as standard.[54]

Sellers whose products are not eminently distinguishable have other motives to promote industrywide standards. They may, for example, want to eliminate "fly-by-nighters," not only to enhance the long-term welfare of the industry, but also to immediately increase their own sales. Efficient high quality producers may also want to use industrywide standards to differentiate their products from those of other established firms. On the other hand, sellers of possibly lower quality items may try to block the standards, or write them low enough so their products receive a similar high grade.

Sellers may also desire standardization on equity grounds, to prevent a situation of continuing product debasement where the cleverest cheater, or the least responsible manfuacturer, receives a competitive advantage. Standards in this case could also benefit society by preventing the elimination of low cost but "responsible" producers, by refocusing competition more on efficiency in production rather than on the ability to disguise quality deterioration.

An interesting case study of sellers working together to create industrywide standards and to limit adulteration is provided by the history of yard lumber size standards. The lumber industry is composed of many small sellers, with little product differentiation among proximate firms, but with some regional differences, and numerous competing and largely regional trade associations (e.g., North Carolina Pine Association, Pacific Coast Lumber Manufacturers Association, Southern Cypress Manufacturers Association, etc.). By the 1920s many associations had promulgated standards. These uniform specifications and quality assurances usually increased regional sales, and also tended to promote standardization by other associations competing for the same business. While the association standards were a vast improvement over the quality assertions of individual mills, much buyer confusion remained. With little coordination among regional groups, there emerged nationally virtually as many different standards as there were trade associations.[55]

Even the dimensions of the commonly purchased 1″ and 2″ width softwood board varied markedly between regions, due to differences in allowances for surfacing and permittable moisture content. Additionally, because of high transport costs, costs related to the actual size of the lumber, there existed a strong incentive for both individual and trade association size adulteration. The two-inch board began gradually to erode, until by 1920 its most common size was 1-5/8″.[56]

While buyers were not happy with the situation they were unable to organize and bring sufficient pressure to force uniform standards upon the industry and end the adulteration. Sellers, generally lacking major differentiation advantages, (especially those that size standardization could erase) probably favored, on equity grounds alone, national standards which should contribute "to the sound, honest and efficient conduct of the lumber trade on the highest plane of integrity, economy and service."[57] They might also have seen some interindustry advantages from "a uniform system, so to speak of 'weights and measures' in the lumber trade similar, in its benefits and convenience, to those prevailing in other industries."[58]

The consensual agreement generally needed for standardization, however, can require a great deal of time and effort, and it may well be true that without the threat of governmental interference and the encouragement of a governmental agency, voluntary national standards would not have emerged in the twenties in the lumber industry. There was then, however, sufficient fear of governmental action to produce a constructive program of industry standards that "would bury public agitation for government regulation."[59] Additionally, the Department of Commerce, headed by Herbert Hoover, not only strongly supported but actually sponsored various lumber conferences at which industry-wide standards were eventually hammered out.[60]

Reaching a consensus was by no means a simple task, and the "Battle of the Thirty-Second" (i.e., should the inch board be 25/32" or 26/32") made industry headlines. Enforcement of the resulting national standard was not easy, an inspection service was found to be impractical, and by 1956 3/4" had become the most common inch board thickness and was adopted as the new standard. By 1964 strong proposals for a 5/8 inch board were being made.[61]

The argument for this further reduction in the standard is an interesting one. The claim, from a social perspective, is that coordination among buyers is beneficial, and that the one- and two-inch width boards have always represented Schellingesque focal points.[62] These sizes, however, may be slightly larger than technically necessary for many tasks. (There is some dispute over this point.) The standard size reduction can thus reduce costs without harming performance, while at the same time maintaining the natural saliency of the nominal "inch board."[63]

In the 1970s there have been attempts to further reduce the 2 by 4 from 1-5/8" x 3-5/8" to 1-1/2" x 3-1/2". Some representatives of the plumbing, heating, and cooling industry argued that this would cause interchangeability problems with pipes, etc. used in homebuilding.[64]

From the standpoint of the lumber industry, of course, the continued collective deterioration could increase joint profits. Industry demand might be characterized by a quantity (board feet) and quality (thickness) dimension. Quantity demanded is then a function of price per quantity, and industrywide quality. At a given price, which may or may not be a competitively determined one, some quality level will maximize industry joint profits in the long run. It usually will not be a Schellingesque round number. Additionally a collective quality adjustment that involves deterioration may be rational due to the short run profits of deception—buyers may not immediately notice the deterioration. Thus present value considerations may make collective quality deterioration a rational strategy even for an industry constrained by free entry to long-run normal profits.

Information, Risk Reduction, and Oligopoly. Some so-called standards are little more than industrywide surveys of current practice. A trade association gathers information on sales by various specifications and may publish those most prevalent as informal standards. Such information can have the effect of further promoting a common pattern of production, of helping to create implicit standards. This action is often welcomed by sellers as part of the trade association's function of information gathering, reducing the cost of individual firms separately attempting to obtain some information about competitors. It should be noted that the information provided by the association is used to create standards only if so desired by sellers, and most generally, when buyers are expert, already buying by specification. Given very knowledgable buyers, sellers are often willing to further aid them by helping formulate some standard specifications.

Sellers may favor standards when their absence increases the risk of costly misunderstandings and disputes. At the turn of the century, for example, growth of the electric industry was being retarded by frequent and expensive litigation caused by the lack of generally accepted measurement and minimum quality standards.[65] In 1905 the National Bureau of Standards reported "numerous cases of dispute regarding the quality of construction materials,"[66] due to the inadequacy of standardization in the building materials industries. In such cases as these, there is some incentive for sellers to cooperate together to create industrywide measurement and often minimum quality standards.

Manufacturers sometimes find standards useful in reducing risk by limiting liability. A single producer's argument that his product was neither unsafe nor unsound is much more persuasive if it can be shown that the item met current industrywide quality standards. While the standard itself is generally held inadmissable, most courts permit testimony as to the provisions of a standard as evidence of the prevailing practices in an industry.[67] With respect to major safety codes, sellers and insurance companies have been known to take the position that contracts do not require repair of even major defects unless they are discovered by the *specific* inspection techniques laid down by the code.[68]

While sellers may favor standards, then, because they lessen liability and decrease dispute costs, it must be emphasized that these potential problems are normally important only when buyers are large and expert. Such problems are generally small for final goods producers, since consumers may lack a precise understanding of what can properly be expected from the product, and the threat of bad publicity, costly litigation or significantly decreased sales is often minimal. These specific seller incentives for standards, therefore, are largely confined to producers goods industries.

Sellers may favor standards that tend to increase stability among themselves. The measurement standards of the Association of Home Appliance Manufacturers, for example, identify those aspects of quality upon which competition will focus.[69] Early measurement and testing standards in the farm machinery industry performed a similar function.[70] The standards tend to make life easier for the manufacturer, to reduce risk and uncertainty by making quality competition somewhat more predictable. This potential benefit from standards is most likely to be recognized by oligopolists, whose profits can be noticeably affected by the actions of specific rivals.

Minimum standards can also help enforce tacit industrywide quality agreements. For example, if the demand for quality is very inelastic, standards can help eliminate lower quality items from the market which might decrease total profits. (The delayed introduction of airline coach service and the small automobile provide examples where major firms probably feared that profits would drop due to lower quality alternatives.) While, from a social viewpoint, standards are often written too low in order to obtain industrywide consensus,[71] this situation provides a clear case where too high standards could emerge.

Complements, and the Vertical Line of Production. Sellers like complements to be inexpensive and of high quality, for this increases the demand for their product. Industrywide quality standards can help in both these areas, by reducing information costs, coordinating demand, and perhaps limiting adulteration. Standards for complements may be especially beneficial to sellers by identifying and reducing the number of "substandard" items which might reduce overall consumer utility, and could even injure seller reputation if consumers cannot properly assess the cause of malfunctions or other problems.

Automotive products provide some classic examples of items manufactured and sold to the consumer by varying industries, but used conjointly in the final product. Automobile manufacturers have an incentive to help insure that consumers receive excellent information about complementary products, to write standards for a product such as brake fluid, where substandard quality could dangerously reduce braking effectiveness. They have an incentive to create minimum oil standards. They may also have a mutual interest with, say, the gasoline industry, to engage in cooperative research to help adapt the fuel to the engine, the engine to the fuel.[72]

Gas and gas appliances are conjointly used complements, and gas utilities have provided the principal impetus behind the standardization of gas appliances.[73] The American Gas Association, representing the vast majority of gas distribution and transmission companies, has long "been concerned about the safety and durability of gas-utilizing appliances, since they are the medium through which our product is sold."[74] The AGA has been involved in the formal standards program for gas appliances and accessories since 1925, sponsoring the writing of safety, durability, and performance standards. Substantial governmental concern over the safety aspects of appliances provided further impetus for the standardization program in the twenties. Currently, in many areas AGA sponsored safety standards are mandatory, having been adopted as law by local authorities.[75]

A firm near the beginning of a vertical chain of production, *certeris paribus*, likes those later in line to sell high quality items at low prices. The more items sold there means, generally, larger demand for the suppliers products, and increased prices and profits. Firms selling producers goods may thus favor quality standards for its buyers products as one way of improving their own market. A group of powerful and organized sellers might be able to insure that the desired standardization actually takes place, particularly, we suspect, if those later in line are numerous, weak, and unorganized.

Examples of firms writing quality standards for those later in the production chain are not very common. Steel and rubber companies, for example, do not write automobile standards, or even specify bike quality; copper firms do not write pot standards; lumber companies do not specify paper quality, or paper firms book quality. The aluminum ingot manufacturers, however, have played a role in writing some standard specifications for fabrications and end products, such as aluminum siding.[76] Automobile and oil companies, of course, try to impose service standards on their particular franchises.

Anticompetitive Motives. Sellers may use standards to decrease competition, by limiting competition among established firms, or by handicapping particular rivals or potential entrants. Standards can limit both price and quality competition among existing firms by facilitating implicit oligopolistic coordination, or even explicit price-fixing and restrictive withholding agreements. Standards not only tend to coordinate buyer demand, but also, of course, can coordinate sellers' price and product policies.

A somewhat ludicrous example of the use of terminology standards to help limit product competition occurred in 1958 when the International Air Transport Association met in plenary session to create a standard definition for the term "sandwich."[77] Uniform treatment of extras in steel,[78] and minimum quality standards for cement,[79] have helped limit competitive pricing and product behavior in those industries. In general, standard specifications and grading, while they may provide increased information to purchasers, can also pave the way for agreements among producers on a price/quality structure that yields high industry profits. From the producer's perspective, therefore, while grading of, say, tires may decrease product differentiation advantages, grades may also facilitate the oligopolistic coordination needed for joint profit maximization.

Those standards attacked by antitrust authorities as integral parts of price-fixing agreements have generally been straight forward standards for uniformity.[80] Minimum quality standards have been more associated with antitrust action involving restrictive withholding arrangements. In the *Standard Sanitary* case, for example, it was held that standards had helped to illegally eliminate inferior "seconds" from the market. [81] In the *Carpet Manufacturers* consent degree, agreements to make only the standard item were specifically prohibited as tending to limit competition.[82] And in the famous *Trenton Potteries* case, the defendant association was charged with seeking to exclude second grade pottery from the market.[83]   In general, under the U.S. antitrust laws, agreements to withhold, along with price-fixing agreements, have been treated as per se illegal. Laws, of course, usually do not completely eradicate all the outlawed activity.

Standards can also be used to handicap certain rivals, or actually exclude them from the market. At the 1967 Small Business Hearings, for example, numerous small firms testified to the exclusionary effect of specific standards. Watts Regulator Company complained of a conspiracy within the American Gas Association approval requirements committee to unfairly discriminated against its product.[84] Largo Co. claimed that a large manufacturer had obtained an amendment to the Uniform Plumbing Code forbidding the use of perfectly acceptable water coolers such as those made by Largo.[85] And the APS plastic pipe manufacturers aired their grievances concerning provisions in local building codes prohibiting the use of non-steel pipes.[86]

Standards can have the greatest exclusionary impact when a seal of approval gains importance in a market, or when, as frequently occurs in the construction field, the standard becomes codified into law. The potential for exclusion is significantly increased when the standard has design or material requirements, rather than being based on performance criteria. Thus wrought brass doorknobs were effectively barred from certain markets because HUD adopted standards requiring doorknobs of cast brass.[87] Plastic products have similarly been denied access to markets because construction codes were written for more traditional materials, such as iron, steel or glass.[88] While, from a social perspective, performance standards are clearly superior to design or material specifications, many standards still contain specific material requirements. The explanation, however, is often less one of anticompetitive intent than of inadequate ability. The technology simply may not be available to either set out the performance required in terms that can be measured, or to carry out the tests needed to evaluate performance. In many areas, good performance standards are impossible (or to use economists jargon, too costly) to write.

It is probably in the area of international trade that the exclusionary effect of standards can be most pronounced. Where standards are increasingly international, such as in cinematography, international exchange is facilitated.[89] In other areas, however, such as electrical equipment, differences in national standards can create high barriers for foreign producers to overcome.[90] Since differing national standards can increase entry barriers, it may behoove efficient manufacturers, producing for export, to help create acceptable international standards. Even better for exporters may be the adoption of their specific standards by foreign nations. Germany, for example, (to our dismay) has been very successful in the promotion of its standards for Latin America, where indigenous standards are still rare.[91] (A country's desire to promote its own standards to new nations or the International Organization for Standardization often leads to a flurry of standards activity designed to improve and upgrade domestic standards.)[92]

While exporters may favor international standardization, domestic producers desiring protection usually prefer unique national standards that handicap foreign sellers. In a U.S. antitrust case, for example, the government charged (unsuccessfully) that domestic producers of asbestos-cement pipe had created standards specifically designed to eliminate competition from foreign manufacturers.[93]

Overall, antitrust in the United States has never dealt severely with voluntary standardization. Standardization activities have been held illegal only in a few instances where they were used to foster a price-fixing scheme. Lower court judges have generally been more impressed by the economic benefits of standards rather than their possible exclusionary effects. While some sellers, fearing prosecution, may have refrained from the cooperative efforts generally needed to produce industrywide standards, in reality, antitrust has always posed only the mildest threat to the drafting and implementation of standards. This means, of course, that blind reliance on antitrust to prevent the anticompetitive abuses potential in standardization may be manifestly misplaced.[94]

International standards and the antitrust aspects of standards are only touched upon in this book. For a few additional sources concerning these topics, see #95 in the Notes Section.

EFFECT OF STANDARDS

The analysis concerning the incentive for standardization should have again served to emphasize that there is no automatic mechanism to insure that any standards will be created, even if they would prove highly beneficial. This is perhaps particularly true in highly competitive markets. Furthermore, there is no reason to expect that when socially beneficial minimum standards are created they will be set at optimal levels. Standards writing is often a quasipolitical process, involving negotiation, bargaining, and compromise among a variety of interests. It is highly unlikely that any emerging standard will prove ideal from some social perspective.

In the preceding section the incentives for standardization were examined, in part looking at the relationship between market structure and the desire (and ability) to create standards. It was emphasized that the impetus generally came from the buyer side, though sellers had a number of motives to promote standardization. In general, however, sellers with particular product differentiation advantages oppose the creation of industrywide quality standards.

This part of the book mentions briefly the related converse effect of standards on markets. It is clear that standards can profoundly affect markets, influencing market structure, conduct and performance. For example, by coordinating demand, standards can change production patterns, thus altering the choices available to any individual consumer. The very fact that there are these "externalities," that what one buyer purchases affects the cost and availability of specific items for others, is, of course, a fundamental reason why buyers demand such standards.

As there are many motives for standards, so too can the effects of standards vary widely. Some performance standards, for instance, can decrease search costs, minimize brand distinctions, and lower entry barriers. Design standards, on the other hand, sometimes raise barriers and impede innovation. From a social viewpoint, standards can have beneficial or deleterious affects. Many standards have elements of both.

Where buyers promote standards, we can usually anticipate that the market effects will prove beneficial. This is particularly true in the case of final goods, for American economists tend largely to equate economic performance with consumer well-being. Consumer created standards could increase information, decrease search and unit production costs, and increase competition, benefits which can greatly exceed the costs of creation. Virtually all buyer-created standards are, however, written for producers' goods. Here the case for standards is somewhat less clear-cut since purchasing firms have an incentive to hurt their own competitors. (The assumption is that consumers have little desire to harm each other.) Organized buyers may be able to create standards that put disorganized purchasers at a small competitive disadvantage. The potential problem, however, does not appear very great. It is difficult, for example, to discover instances of firms unfairly disadvantaged due to the existence of standard specifications written for purchased products.

Where sellers promote standards, the market effects are more uncertain. Standards written to facilitate price-fixing or to exclude competitors are usually inimicable to social well-being, whereas standards written to prevent adulteration are generally helpful. Standards to increase market stability could well be either. An interesting conclusion is that, regarding exclusively the area of standardization, market performance is often improved by the existence of market power in complementary industries, or along the vertical chain of production or, of course, among buyers.

Where goods are graded, grades written, and products tested by some competent and independent authority, we may expect a number of results. Two competitive effects are the lessening of those scale purchasing economies caused by the cost of obtaining product quality information, and the decrease in quality assurance-product differentiation advantages, often making small concerns more competitive and tending to decrease seller concentration. Established firms with brand advantages will thus often oppose grading proposals. Whether, from society's viewpoint, particular goods should be graded is a complex question, requiring the comparison of costs and benefits of this form of product information provision with other methods (e.g., brand names). This is a question that has not been focused upon in this book.

Chapter Eight

Standards Creation in the United States

In contrast to most other countries, formal standards writing in the United States is largely a private affair. Nearly 400 distinct and private organizations administer the creation of voluntary standards in the United States. Of the 14,000 formal industrywide standards in 1964, less then 3 per cent had been written under governmental auspices.[1]

In the United States, standards are written primarily by engineering societies, such as the American Society of Mechnical Engineers (ASME) or the Institute of Electrical Electronics Engineers (IEEE), and by trade associations, such as the Business Equipment Manufacturers Association or the American Petroleum Institute. There are also a number of less easily categorizable institutions which play an important role in standards creation, such as the American Society for Testing and Materials (ASTM) and the National Fire Protection Association (NFPA). Formal coordination of the potentially overlapping activities of the standards writing organizations is provided by the American National Standards Institute (ANSI), the national clearinghouse of standards.

While a wide array of engineering societies and trade associations create standards, the bulk of the activity is performed by only a few organizations. In 1964, three institutions, the American Society for Testing and Materials, the Society of Automotive Engineers (SAE), and the Aerospace Industries Association (AIA) wrote over one-half of all voluntary industrywide standards. Another fifteen organization prepared 20 per cent of the then existing standards. Although standards are not homogeneous in nature—some being of much broader scope than others—it is still clear that standards creation in the United States is a highly "concentrated" activity. Additionally, the central clearinghouse of standards has been rapidly increasing its role in standards-making. While only 17 per cent of industrywide standards had been processed by

ANSI's predecessor organization in 1964,[2] today the large majority of standards are channeled through this powerful institution.

TRADE ASSOCIATIONS

Typically, the trade association is a nonprofit organization of independent business competitors formed to promote the members' interests in a variety of ways. One important function of the trade association is to serve as a central clearinghouse for information, gathering and disseminating data on individual firm and industry sales, profits, accidents, etc. The association can also provide aid and advice to its members in a number of areas, such as accounting, marketing, and employee relationships. It may promote joint research, cooperative insurance, patent pooling, institutional advertising, as well as industrywide standards. It is the industry representative with the government, unions, and the public. Overall, the association role is to improve the position of the industry in the economy, and in society.[3]

Providing a forum for standards creation is just one of the many services provided by the trade association. The nature and importance of this function, of course, varies greatly among associations, depending in large part on the incentives of the firms in the industry. The National Association of Hosiery Manufacturers, for example, has helped create a uniform measurement system for pantyhose.[4] The American Gas Association writes standards for complementary products.[5] The Comics Magazine Association of America has its Comic Book Code of Ethics.[6] On the other hand, there are often strong vested interests opposing particular standards. The trade associations in drugs and cosmetics, for example, might be committing suicide should they attempt to promote minimum industrywide quality standards, which could diminish the product differentiation advantages of established firms.

Even if small concerns without product differentiation advantages desired such standards, they would probably not get written. For while the trade association may bring more potential benefits to the small firm, providing needed advice and coordination, it does seem as if the big producers should generally dominate the association. The view of the big company is always represented at meetings, a view which is "coordinated" and expert, a view backed by financial power. Additionally, the threat by the big company to leave the association may prove decisive, for the association can then no longer speak for the entire industry.

As Congressman John Dingall has argued:

> ... the trade association is not entirely free to thwart the determined will of its largest contributors. It may be that the smaller business members of a trade association contribute more in the aggregate than the larger units. But the smaller units are typically

not coalesced and lack the technical advice to understand whether or how they are being technically misled. Two or three very large units in an industry trade association may contribute such a substantial portion of the total annual revenue that indication on their part that they might resign will quickly bring the trade association to heel. For example, three or four years ago, the Weyerhaeuser Company and Georgia-Pacific Corporation announced their resignation from the Douglas Fir Plywood Association. The matter about which each was unhappy was, I am told, quickly remedied and the resignations voided.[7]

Since standards writing generally requires organization, whether and what exact standards are created may depend, in part, on trade association membership. If, for example, the association is composed of companies with horizontal and no vertical relationships, it may be more difficult for firms to help write standards for goods later along in the chain of production.

While the association exists to serve its members, like most institutions it may develop some independent goals of its own. The trade association, for example, receives different information and feels different pressures than its client companies, and its monopoly position allows it some autonomous power. Sometimes, like the Association of Home Appliance Manufacturers,[8] it can be found promoting standards about which its members are, at best, uncertain. Indeed, it might be argued that many associations are, in part, promoting themselves via standards certification, or recognized seals of approval.

ENGINEERING SOCIETIES

Sometimes the forum for standards creation is provided by engineering societies. Unlike the medical profession, engineers do not have a single major professional association which has acted to enhance the economic position of its members. Instead there has been a tendency toward the "Balkanization" of the occupation. There are presently over one hundred engineering societies, the twenty-three important national institutions containing some 650,000 members.[9] The principal societies researched for this section of this book were the Society of Automotive Engineers (SAE: 27,000 members), the American Society of Mechanical Engineers (ASME: 55,000 members), the Institute of Electrical and Electronics Engineers (IEEE: 137,000 members) and the American Society of Civil Engineers (ASCE: 63,000 members).[10]

Membership in the societies is individual, with membership stratified according to years of education and practice, and by accomplishments. Of the four societies, the SAE seems most prone to admit people without engineering degrees. In the local Boston chapter, for example, there are bus fleet operators, owners of wholesale automotive equipment stores, tire representatives, etc.[11]

Officers of the societies are essentially selected rather than elected. Generally it is a matter of finding good men who are willing to spend the time.[12]

The principal function of these societies is education. Their main role is to aid in the advancement and dissemination of engineering knowledge, primarily through journal publications and chapter meetings.[13] These societies affect not only the engineer's continuing education, but also his formal education through membership in the Engineers Council for Professional Development (ECPD). ECPD accreditation of schools is generally accepted for purposes of the state licensing of engineers. Thus ECPD most powerfully influences formal education by upgrading the quality of the curricula of the weaker schools.[14]

These societies can improve the engineering labor market, facilitating the recruitment of employees.[15] Generally, however, the societies seem to play little formal role in recruitment. Informally, though, through society publications and at society meetings, the individual engineer quite naturally gains some information about pay and working conditions elsewhere. The ASME, for example, maintains no "employment service." While for many years the Society cooperated with other professional engineering organizations in the operation of the Engineering Societies Personnel Service, Inc., the operation was terminated primarily because so few of the Society members used the service. Companies do place classified advertisements in the principal society publication, *Mechanical Engineering*, and many members use these ads for employment contacts.[16]

The ASME, ASCE, IEEE, and SAE are all nonprofit, tax-exempt organizations, and they jealously guard that status. Thus they do not officially lobby; their influence on legislation is exerted primarily via their expertise. They can unofficially ask to be asked to testify at various hearings, or they can volunteer their services elsewhere. In 1970, for example, the ASME offered to provide the New England states "with a no cost review of plans for public works in almost any field where unbiased engineering opinion or recommendation can be of value to the administration."[17]

Standards creation is often an important function of an engineering society. Among the societies there are quite different philosophies regarding this activity. The ASCE, for example, is not really a standard-setting organization, though its members will sit with standard-setting groups, as local building code committees.[18] The IEEE does create definitional and measurement standards, as well as standard test procedures, but it generally refuses to "put in numbers."[19] The IEEE believes that when a standard deals with economic and commercial matters, standard making should be left to a trade association such as the National Electrical Manufacturers Association. One IEEE standard, for instance, is concerned with test procedures for measuring the noise of rotating electrical machinery, a technical and scientific problem. "The standard does not concern itself with stating what levels may be expected of normal commercial apparatus.

How noisy a motor should be is a more appropriate subject for a trade association,"[20] The SAE and the ASME both "put in numbers," and in this sense act more like trade associations than either the IEEE or ASCE.

As in the case of trade associations, it appears that corporations, (generally major corporations) dominate the standards-writing process within engineering societies. While both the SAE and ASME claim that their members serve entirely as individuals and not as company representatives, this seems more formality than fact. The engineer in a large corporation has little professional independence. Sociologists have explained that the relationship of the engineer with his superiors is better characterized by the norm of obedience than by the norm of service (which is typical of a professional) or the norm of autonomy (which is typical of a scientist).[21] The salaried engineer cannot speak with true independence on many issues, particularly those which have become "sensitive." His own success, in a measure, is proof of his ability to view things from the point of view of his own self-interest.[22]

The company also plays a major role in the direct relationship of the corporate engineer with his professional society. The company often pays the membership dues,[23] and generally provides paid time off for meetings, besides paying the individual's way. As a vice president of Phillips Petroleum said: "It seems obvious that the average engineer in industry cannot participate in meetings on a regional or national basis without industry support. I feel that I cannot overemphasize the importance of this point."[24]

Nor are the engineering societies themselves independent and largely free from the powerful influence of industry. Industry contributions, for example, substantially underwrite the entire standardization and research activities of the SAE.[25] The ASME reports only 35 per cent of its annual income comes from membership dues (sometimes paid by the industry) while 59 per cent came from advertising in *Mechanical Engineering*, and also publications sales including codes, standards, and research.[26]

The 1929 National Industrial Conference Board survey of standards accurately sums up the situation: "Practically all of the engineering societies are in close touch with, or generally reflect, the corporate and trade association point of view."[27]

Not only are companies well represented, since most engineers are industry employees, but major firms tend to dominate the standardization meetings. We have already emphasized that it is usually more difficult to coordinate the "small business interest," and that the free rider problem is more prevalent there. It is clear that, compared to the large-scale enterprise, a single small firm finds it relatively more costly to pay the expenses of employees engaged in standards activity. While the trade association could help insure that the interests of the small firm receive adequate representation, the association itself is probably dominated by the major firms.

Other interests generally are not well represented in the engineering society forum. The laborer, for example, may be vitally affected by standards concerning the quality of the tools, machines, and materials he uses, but he is often lacking in technical expertise, and even the expenditure of large funds by the labor organization may not guarantee him adequate representation in organizations dominated by corporations. The AFL-CIO has long argued that it is too heavily outnumbered and outfinanced to have sufficient say in standardization activities. When labor interests are affected, it usually prefers governmental legislation to voluntary standards. Hence the strong backing for the mandatory Occupational Safety and Health Act.[28]

The individual consumer not only lacks the technical expertise needed to work on most standardizing committees, but he is without an organization capable of representing him. Engineering societies do, though, usually make some attempt to secure "public interest" representatives. This generally means asking, but not aiding, independent experts to attend standardization meetings. The token effort is normally not enough. Not only is it difficult to find men who can represent the public well—technical experts with no "conflict of interest"—but such men are usually not adequately renumerated by the public interest they represent.[29]

These factors, combined with the general laissez-faire attitude of government, mean that both the consuming and public interest have little voice in voluntary standardization in the United States. Examination of actual standardization committees indicates that public interest representatives—professors, consultants, government personnel, and representatives from agencies such as Consumers Union, the National Safety Council, or the American Insurance Association—usually comprise only a small minority of the membership. Appendixes B and C analyze in depth the makeup of two particular committees.

It should be stressed that non-industry experts do not always make excellent representatives for the nebulous "public interest." Usually such men are not so aggressive compared to the corporate representatives, and sometimes they actually speak for rather parochial interests, such as those of a specific governmental agency.

Whether standards are written by trade associations or engineering societies is partly a matter of historical precedent. The Automobile Manufacturers Association, for example, creates few standards, in part because of the long standards-writing experience of the SAE. There are also, of course, advantages and disadvantages to the large-scale enterprise from either approach. Using the engineering society route may necessitate relinquishing some small degree of control, but the resulting standards are more likely to appear "unbiased." Moreover, engineering societies provide one vehicle by which different *industries* can get together to conjointly write standard specifications for commonly purchased products.

ASTM, NFPA, AND UL

Probably no discussion of American standards is complete without some mention of the American Society for Testing and Materials (ASTM), the National Fire Protection Association (NFPA), or Underwriters Laboratories (UL). The ASTM is the dominant standards-writing body in America. A nonprofit, technical society, its main work concerns research and standardization in materials. It is specifically interested in the quality and testing of materials, and does not generally become involved in dimensional standardization or design problems. The ASTM *Book of Standards,* containing more than thirty-four volumes and 22,000 pages, deals with such areas as steel piping materials; copper and copper alloys; cement, lime, and gypsum; gaseous fuels; general testing methods, etc. By providing a broad forum for materials standardization, the ASTM has served an important coordination function, preventing much overlapping and duplication of activities by diverse groups in this general area.[30]

The ASTM contains both individual and organizational membership. Unlike the SAE and ASME, who advocate the fiction that members serve entirely as individuals, the ASTM actually encourages the various conflicting interests in standardization questions to represent those interests. The ASTM operates under stricter procedures then do most other standardizing bodies. Committee membership, for example, is balanced between producers, buyers, and general interest groups, with a producer-oriented voting strength not to exceed 50 per cent. Technical committee chairmanship is restricted to a member in the nonproducing sector.[31] These and other ASTM procedures make it *more* likely, in the words of a district court judge, "that results reached by them will be scientifically sound and will represent the general interest."[32]

The National Fire Protection Association is a nonprofit organization whose principal functions are educating the public to the hazards of fire, and creating engineering standards and recommended practices to reduce the loss of life and property by fire. The NFPA has over 27,000 individual and organizational members who have written and approved some 200 fire related standards, filling more than 9,000 pages. The standards cover such general areas as flammable liquids, building construction, transportation, sprinklers, and alarms. A large number are used for insurance purposes, and many are adopted in federal, state, and municipal regulations.[33]

Underwriters' Laboratories, Inc., a not-for-profit institution sponsored by the American Insurance Association, is one of the oldest and most respected certification laboratories in the United States. While UL is most noted for its role in the prevention of electrical and fire hazards in the home, its focus is more broadly safety oriented, encompassing such areas as theft and accident prevention. UL testing and certification procedures include inspection follow-ups of the factories where listed devices are manufactured. UL also writes some standards, especially standard test procedures. These are often submitted to the American National Standards Institute for national adoption.[34]

A potential problem of UL is that since its revenues depend in part on the number of products voluntarily submitted for tests, there is a tendency to write standards that maximize revenues or profits, rather than consumer well-being. Standards may often be set somewhat lower than the socially optimal level.[35]

ANSI

Voluntary standards are sometimes categorized as being created on four distinct levels: (1) within a company, (2) by a trade association or technical society, (3) through a national standardizing body, or (4) on an international scale.[36] This book has ignored the first level, and focused on the second. In the United States, the American National Standards Institute occupies the third level, acting as the *only* recognized nongovernmental entity in the field. ANSI's predecessor organization, the American Engineering Standards Committee was created in 1918 by the ASTM and four engineering societies (mining, mechanical, civil, and electrical). The governmental departments of Commerce, War, and Navy were cofounders. In 1928 the name was changed to the American Standards Association. In the mid-sixties the organization was known briefly as the United States of America Standards Institute. Today the ANSI federation is composed of over 160 technical, professional, and trade associations, along with more than 1,000 company members. ANSI's principal functions are to serve as a standards coordinator—to eliminate duplication, overlapping, unnecessary conflicts, and variations in standards—and to act as a central clearinghouse for information on standards. ANSI also holds the U.S. membership in the International Organization of Standards (IOS).[37]

ANSI both approves standards and provides a forum for their creation. Since the 1965 LaQue report, the Institute has grown rapidly, in part by inducing principal standard-writing organizations, like the SAE, to submit their standards for approval. ASTM spokesmen have sometimes argued that ANSI's desire to increase its role in standardization has led it to give blanket approval to standards whose creation procedures were far less than ideal.[38]

ANSI is, of course, dominated by major firms. It is largely financed by the large-scale enterprise; most of the standards approved are written by organizations dominated by large-scale enterprises. Smaller companies have long viewed the Institute with some suspicion.[39] Consumers have recently been given token representation in ANSI via the creation of a Consumer Council. But the council's role is purely advisory, and is largely composed of (buying) industry personnel rather than spokesmen for the ultimate consumer.[40] Even in those areas where final good standards are promulgated, the consumer has little real voice in determining standards. Consumers Union reports, for example, that, as with its experience with other standard writing bodies, its suggestions have consistently been voted down, overwhelmed by the "consensus" of industry.[41]

The consensus principle is crucial in the development of American standards. Explains ANSI: "A consensus does not necessarily mean unanimous acceptance. Votes are weighted rather than counted. A weighty objection of one important organization may outweigh all other affirmative votes. Or a number of negative votes of groups that are only distantly concerned with the subject matter may be discounted in the face of affirmative votes of parties that are vitally affected by the standard." Observed James Ridgeway in the *New Republic*: "This means just about anything one might want it to mean, and in an organization weighted toward the interests of big business, it suggests that industry will get pretty much what it wants."[42]

Analyzing ANSI's operating procedure, lawyer Marian Opala has argued that other potential problems include its secrecy, the lack of separation between standards-creation activities and the review of standards, and between standards review and the raising of funds.[43]

NATIONAL BUREAU OF STANDARDS

Aside from the creation of purchase specifications, government involvement in voluntary standardization has come largely through the National Bureau of Standards. Currently there are three major areas of NBS activity. The first concerns the custody, maintenance, and development of the basic National Measurement System. The second deals with materials research. The bureau is responsible for the development and sale of standard reference materials used for the accurate calibration of measuring instruments. These two functions involve traceability, with the bureau acting as the primary reference. The third major branch of the NBS is the Institute of Applied Technology, and an important concern here is voluntary product standards, the focus of this book. Other related activities of the bureau include promulgation of mandatory flammable fabric standards, provision of technical assistance to local governments in the area of weights and measures, computer services research, etc. Overall, the National Bureau of Standards functions as a science research facility for the federal government.[44]

The voluntary standards program of the bureau reached its heyday in the 1920s when Herbert Hoover was Secretary of Commerce. Emphasizing the "elimination of waste" in industry (X-efficiency) Hoover and the NBS pushed hard for simplification of products as well as the creation of minimum standards where appropriate. Since that time, the bureau's role in voluntary standardization has become more passive.

In the 1960s, only 3 per cent of all voluntary standards were written under Commerce Department (NBS) procedures. This meant principally that the NBS provided the ground rules for standardization, ground rules not fundamentally different from those of many private associations. The bureau didn't try to force standardization, or to help create optimal standards. It viewed itself principally as a catalyst for standards creation, with a negative function of insuring that standards were not written that would prove inimical to the public interest.[45]

In the postwar period, U.S. government participation in voluntarily standardization has been far less than the involvement of governments in virtually all other developed countries.[46] And currently, following the recommendations of the LaQue report, the NBS is attempting to phase itself out of this entire area. The bureau is trying to transfer all its activities to the private sector, making the Commerce Department route to voluntary standardization a safety-valve supplement rather than any kind of competing alternative to private standardization forums. However, over four hundred Bureau employees still participate on private standards committees (though rarely on those of trade associations).[47]

STANDARDS AND GOVERNMENT POLICY

The government has taken a largely laissez-faire attitude toward voluntary standardization in the United States. Not only has it been relatively uninvolved with the standardization process, but it has not collected good data on the pervasiveness of standards. Nor, it seems, has anyone else. There is little statistical information on standards—the degree to which they are followed or used, the number that subsequently find their way into mandatory regulation, etc. Voluntary standards have grown like Topsy, and from all evidence, that growth currently appears to be accelerating, with gradually greater emphasis being placed in the consumer goods area.

The increased attention paid to the development of final goods standards can be credited in large part to the emergence of consumerism as a political force. Consumers, however, have not created consumer-oriented institutions to write standards for final goods. Instead, existing standardizing bodies, already dominated by industry, merely took on the added task of creating more consumer goods standards.

The control of standards-writing organizations by big business in the United States is entirely consistent with the hypotheses and arguments presented in previous chapters. Standards generally are created when desired by major firms, and rarely if opposed by them (unless other large concerns force standardization). When quality standards are created, we can predict that they will be written at levels that help established, dominant firms maintain their dominance.

Since this situation seems far less than ideal, intelligent government policy could probably lead to improved results. For consumers, for example, government could perhaps write mandatory standards for more products, for ambulances, say, as well as for certain aspects of automobiles. Mandatory standards may be required since with unorganized, often uninformed consumers, voluntary standards might never be used. Government could, of course, help promote consumer information in other ways, not only by Truth-in-Lending type legislation, but also possibly with more "counter-ads." Probably most importantly, government could help organize consumers, and might even aid in the creation of consumer dominated standards writing organizations.

Within the current standards system, government should at least insure the adequacy of standard-writing procedures. As Acting Undersecretary of Commerce, J. Herbert Hollomon proposed some procedural guidelines it might prove socially beneficial for a standards-writing institution to follow. They are, principally: (a) balanced committees: (b) an open process; (c) the publicizing of results with explanations, including identification of opposition, and affording the opportunity for dissenting comments before the issuance of the standard; (d) appeal procedure to an independent impartial professional staff; and (e) an annual report evaluating procedures and results. At the House Small Business Hearings, Hollomon, a standards expert, was asked what per cent of private standards writing organizations had such procedures. He replied: "I know of no standards-writing body personally, although there may be some. I simply know of none that would meet all those criteria."[48]

Even Hollomon's criteria seems less than optimal. Like virtually all standards experts, Hollomon argues that committees should be balanced among those affected—producers, distributors, users, the public interest, etc.—and that some consensus among them is required before standards can be promulgated. Theoretically, however, from a social standpoint, it would seem that buyers or users should be the principal voting members of standardizing committees. For example, where minimum standards provide information and coordinate demand, where perhaps there is some cost-quality tradeoff, the necessary tradeoff information should be provided (probably by producers) and then buyers alone, albeit collectively, should attempt to make appropriate choice. Ideally, for final goods standards, as the consumer is king in the marketplace, so correspondingly should he be king within the standards committees. Of course, where there are "third person problems," clearly the public interest should also have a voice.

Without strong government action, there is no present reason for industry to relinquish its power within the standards committees. When standards are created, the severity of the economic problems caused by big business domination of the standardizing process varies greatly with the type of standard under consideration. For definition or measurement standards, for example, and even standards for uniformity, the problems are not so serious as for minimum quality standards written by sellers, or for those concerning areas where externalities are prevalent. Ideally, rather than insuring that all standardizing committees follow a uniform set of rules, it might be better if the rules varied somewhat depending on the type of standard being produced, whether it is expected to become codified into law, etc.

Chapter Nine

Summary and Conclusions

Economists, in fact all academicians, have virtually ignored the entire area of industrywide standards. The model of perfect competition, with its strict postulates of "perfect" information and naturally homogeneous products, depicts a world where standards are irrelevant. When relaxing the assumptions to permit product heterogeneity, Industrial Organization economists have generally focused on the causes and effects of individual firm product differentiation, rarely considering the possibility of collective action (save for patently illegal purposes). Again, in the newly emerging economics of information field, scholars have paid little attention to the use made of voluntary *industrywide* agreements or standards in decreasing the cost of providing and obtaining accurate product information.

In general, microeconomists have been much more interested in questions concerning price rather than product determination. The present book takes the product as a prime economic variable. It intensively examines one often important factor that can influence product quality, and even product size, in the marketplace—voluntary industrywide standards.

A principal question focused on in this book is under what circumstances standards are likely to be created. (A secondary question concerns whether or not those created will prove optimal by some criteria.) The book discusses the various benefits and costs of standards, and thus the incentive for their creation, relating this to various aspects of market structure. Because of the collective and thus inherently political nature of much standards creation, there is no automatic mechanism to insure that beneficial standards will be created, even—perhaps particularly—in highly competitive industries. The book presents arguments, combined with much supporting evidence, that whether or not standards are likely to be created depends, in part, on the type of standard in question, and on buyer and seller concentration, as well as firm product differentiation.

93

Whether or not standards are created can depend too on the existence of organizations capable of creating acceptable standards (e.g., early automotive standards awaited the formation of the SAE), on trade association leadership (AHAM), individual management philosophy (many "free enterprises" in the toy industry opposed virtually any industrywide quality standards for their products), government policy (Is Herbert Hoover Secretary of Commerce?), rate of product change, and many other factors.

There is, unfortunately, no standard way of classifying (or defining) standards. This book discusses industrywide product standards, and differentiates between two principal types: standards for uniformity, where better or worse is not at issue, but sameness or uniformity is; and quality standards, which categorize products as either "superior" (meeting the standard) or "inferior" (not meeting it). Standards for uniformity can be further divided into the simplification of single products, and standards for two or more conjoint products to enhance interchangeability. In the real world, of course, there is some blurring of these sharp distinctions.

A crucial notion in understanding the benefits of standards is that there are externalities in purchase. What I buy affects what is available to you, and vice versa. Standards, by coordinating demand, can sometimes make us both better off. A conclusion of the analysis is that, in many situations, market power—especially on the buyer side—may be helpful in insuring the creation of beneficial standards.

Single product standards for uniformity are substantially less important in the U.S. economy than either interchangeability or quality standards. A principal possible benefit from single product uniformity standards is that they might help achieve economies of scale in production and distribution. For example, if purchases of individual buyers are small, and if, say, atomistic sellers or distributors find it difficult to unilaterally offer the option of "standard" items at lower price, then by effectively coordinating demand, industrywide standards could allow otherwise unobtainable scale economies.

Formal industrywide single product standards for uniformity should theoretically prove most helpful where both buyers and sellers are small. This is often the situation when atomistic buyers face atomistic sellers. It is in such cases, however, when it is usually most difficult to get the affected parties together to agree on standards. Here the government might play a role. In the 1920s, for example, the government, led by Herbert Hoover, made its major peacetime simplification efforts, achieving beneficial variety reduction in a large number of industries, encompassing products such as nails, files, paint brushes, and lumber. While many of the industries possessed the expected market structure characteristics, it must be emphasized that Department of Commerce simplification efforts were but a part of Hoover's larger program to eliminate waste in industry—to facilitate the functioning of the market even where microeconomic theory would suggest that, in the long run, economic forces might eventually compel the desired increases in efficiency.

The other major potential benefit from single product standards for uniformity is that they can facilitate price comparisons, particularly for final consumers. Here the situation is one where my purchases can affect the profitability of odd-sized containers and size proliferation, making your comparison shopping easier or more difficult. A fundamental purpose of the federal Fair Labelling and Packaging Act was to promote size uniformity by getting producers to limit variety, thus decreasing the cost to consumers of determining the relative prices of competing brands. Today, unit pricing is beginning to provide a sometimes-less-troublesome substitute for these simplification efforts.

The potential economic costs of voluntary simplification are not large. Where standards are voluntary, for example, manufacturers can still produce non-standard items if it is profitable to do so. Probably the major practical problems arising from voluntary simplification efforts are the inherent dangers if producers are agreeing together. It should be noted, for instance, that size standardization makes the creation and enforcement of price-fixing arrangements somewhat easier.

Most standards for uniformity involve some sort of interchangeability. Typewriter and adding machine keyboard standards facilitate the substitution of people and machines, industrywide brick size standards ease replacement problems, and tire and rim, nut and bolt, and bulb and lamp socket standards permit interchange between conjoint products of different suppliers. Standards for uniformity can help achieve scale economies, and, for consumers, help make comparison shopping easier. Interchangeability standards also widen markets. They increase the number of alternative sources of supply, and thus promote competition. Interchangeability standards can lower domestic entry barriers, and decrease search costs. Their general effect on innovative activity is less certain.

For conjoint products, when firms are not manufacturing both commodities, there is frequently an incentive for sellers to create interchangeability standards. Such standards decrease dependence on other specific suppliers, increase sales opportunities, sometimes enhancing the value of the product (as with records and record players). On the other hand, sellers may be reluctant to relinquish a quasi-captive market, and agreeing on standards may prove bothersome, or require leadership that is sometimes lacking. If there were a dominant manufacturer in one line, however, his product would quickly become the pattern for informal standards.

Usually, some important firms produce both parts of conjoint products (razors and blades, staples and staplers). In this situation, major firms generally have strong incentives to oppose industrywide interchangeability standards. The absence of standards helps tie the manufacturers products together, and where tying is profitable, interchangeability standards may prove detrimental to the dominant concerns. We might expect, then, when at least one line is characterized by oligopoly, with the major firms producing in both lines, that socially beneficial interchangeability standards might never be created. However, in virtually all cases, regardless of seller incentives, industrywide standards can be effectively imposed if powerful buyers agree to coordinate their purchases.

Quality standards divide products into categories of better or worse. Like standards for uniformity, the principal virtue of standard specifications is that they serve to coordinate demand. Standard specifications can thus allow scale economies, ease price comparisons and promote price competition, permit quick delivery, and insure future availability. Standard specifications also reduce the product information problem for the buyer. If created by a consensus of diverse and knowledgeable parties, they can be used with some security. The buyer is saved the expense of writing his own specification. Moreover, since standard items have been purchased over time by a large number and variety of users, performance information about them is readily obtainable through observation, personal contacts, trade journals, etc.

A basic benefit of standards is that they neatly package product quality information. Information is an unusual commodity, a somewhat inappropriable non-rival public good. The demand for information is essentially a derived demand, and is met in a variety of ways, none of them ideal. For example, advertising, brand names, personal search, advice from friends, or independent information producers, and specifications are all means of obtaining information. Standard specifications represent yet another, and partially competing method by which product information can be provided.

Economists have just begun to investigate the economics of information. For our purposes, the most interesting model is that presented by Akerlof.[1] It assumes that sellers possess accurate product information, and that buyers lack information on specific products, but know something about average market quality. There are "averaging externalities" in the model—each seller's products influence the product quality that otherwise uninformed buyers expect to receive.

An Akerlof-type model describes a situation that possesses a high potential for adulteration—generally small, individual producers unable to sufficiently differentiate their products, selling goods to buyers who can tell average quality within an industry, but not, before purchase, the quality of a particular producer. In situations with "averaging externalities," producers may have a collective interest to raise or stabilize market quality by creating and certifying standards. The incentive may be especially great if there exists strong interindustry competition.

In the general case, however, major producers tend to oppose industrywide standards. This is particularly true concerning commodity aspects where pronounced product differentiation has been achieved, for standards, by guaranteeing quality on an industrywide basis, eliminate some of the advantages of product differentiation. Normally, when purchases are made by specification, or goods are graded, some of the potential quality assurance advantages derived from large past and present sales disappear, entry is made easier, and small firms are more capable of surviving in the industry.

Buyers are the ones who normally benefit most from standards and force their creation. To compel standardization normally requires a collective action by buyers that is more easily achieved when there are a few principal purchasers. Indeed, when there are a small number of large buyers, there generally exists a great many helpful standard specifications. Conversely, the lack of coordination and organization among atomistic final consumers is the main reason why there are relatively few consumer goods standards.

While sellers generally oppose industrywide standards, there are a number of situations when they have incentives to create them. The problems of adulteration and averaging, and the role standards can play in industrywide quality assurance has already been mentioned. Additionally, by being generally accepted and often used, standards can reduce the risk of costly misunderstandings and may lessen seller liability. Such problems are not usually great, however, unless buyers are already large and powerful. Sellers may also favor voluntary standards that prevent or influence potential mandatory standards imposed by government. Sellers of complements, or products used along the vertical chain of production, may write standards to benefit buyers, and ultimately themselves. Finally, sellers may attempt to create and use standards for anticompetitive purposes—to limit product and price competition among existing firms, or to effectively exclude competitors from the market.

To the extent that standards diminish product differentiation advantages, they make the demand curves facing existing firms more elastic, generally increasing the potency of price competition. This very fact may give oligopoly sellers greater incentive to coordinate their pricing policies, and the standards themselves, by decreasing heterogeneity, facilitate price-fixing arrangements.

While sellers have some incentives to create standards, the analysis indicates that when buyers lack power, socially beneficial standards often may not be written (and detrimental standards may be). Even when beneficial quality standards are created, there is no reason to expect that they will be set at optimal levels. For standards writing generally involves negotiation, bargaining, and compromise among a variety of interests. Such a political process tends to produce workable rather than economically ideal standards.

A rather crude analogy could be drawn between the economist's conception of a free market and town meeting democracy on the one hand, and standards creation and a Republic on the other. In the free market, as in pure democracy, each individual casts his (dollar) vote for policies or goods, whereas for standards creation, as in a Republic, selected representatives make many of the important decisions. In this latter situation, it clearly makes a great deal of difference what interests are represented. This book shows that, in the United States, major firms tend to dominate the standards writing process. This gives them great power in determining not only what standards are created, but exactly what those standards will say.

Relative to small firms, the large-scale concerns possess more than their proportional share of power in the standards creation process, mainly because they are bigger and because smaller concerns are numerous and diverse. Whereas the cost of sending representatives to the standardization meetings is largely independent of firm size, the absolute benefit (or cost) from any particular standard is generally related to sales. In other words, the large firm internalizes more of the collective benefit from standards than does the individual small company. The numerous small firms generally find it difficult to harmonize their somewhat conflicting interests, and singly, any individual concern may correctly conclude that it cannot substantially influence the standards-writing process. Even if a unified "small business interest" were apparent, small firms would still need organization and cooperation to overcome the Mancor Olsen free rider problem.[2] For the consumer, labor or general public interest, which internally lack the requisite technical expertise, the problems of securing adequate representation on the standardizing committees are even more substantial.

Large firm control of the standardizing process can be troublesome, for standards not only help determine the low cost product choices available to small buyers, but can also aid or hurt particular firms. Control of the standardizing process is thus one small way that dominant firms can maintain their dominance. Additionally, all potential problems of standards, including their use for patently illegal and anticompetitive purposes, are heightened if sellers, rather than buyers, dominate the standards committees.

In contrast to the situation prevailing in most advanced countries, direct governmental involvement in the voluntary standardization process of the United States has been rather limited. In the laissez-faire tradition, government has neither been active in, nor underwritten, voluntary standardization efforts. The number of Commerce Department sponsored standards has never been great during the postwar period, and the agency is presently attempting to transfer all such activity to the private sector. Antitrust enforcement of standards has focused almost exclusively on per se violations of the statutes. Direct governmental involvement in voluntary standardization today consists largely of sending representatives to various standards meetings.

The government does influence voluntary standards, of course, through its purchases and writing of its own specifications and through the threat of imposing mandatory standards. This threat has increased in recent years as the government displayed less reluctance to impose standards for a variety of purposes: to ease information problems (FLPA), combat the problems caused by externalities (gas pipeline standards), limit adulteration (FDA peanut butter identity standards), improve product quality (auto safety standards), and so on. Ideally, the government might play an even more active role in the promotion of beneficial voluntary standards (e.g., bumper height standards) and it should at least do more to insure that difficult-to-organize interest groups receive more adequate representation in the standardizing process.

As a whole, this book has attempted to depict the role played by voluntary industrywide product standards in our economy. Standards were first classified, and their benefits, as well as some costs, were explained. The incentives and abilities to create standards were then examined and an attempt was made to relate these to market structure characteristics. A few perscriptions for public policy emerged from this discussion.

In the industrial organization structure-conduct-performance tricot-omy, we might say that standards setting is a form of market conduct, influencing and influenced by structural elements (e.g., concentration, product differentiation) as well as other elements of conduct (e.g., tying, advertising). Standards affect market performance attributes directly—such as the general level of product quality, or the rate and pattern of product change—as well as indirectly through their influence on structure and conduct.

Although undeniably important, industrywide voluntary product standards have received little attention from scholars. There is scant systematic data on the subject, though information was obtainable from an interesting array of nonacademic sources. Perhaps the greatest difficulty encountered, however, was that discussion of standards involved a number of highly important concepts dealt with quite inadequately in the literature. These include information, product quality, externalities, and collective action. It is in such areas that productive microeconomic research is clearly possible.

Appendix A

Single Product Standards for Uniformity: Economy of Scale Benefits

The purpose of this appendix is to use payoff matrices to formalize the potential economy of scale benefits from single product standards for uniformity. Assume that average costs of production decrease over a range, and the purchases of a single buyer are too small to realize all potential economies. Also assume that sellers either lack the incentive or ability to offer the choice of reduced variety at lowered cost. Begin, for simplicity, with a market composed of a monopoly seller and two buyers, each buyer ordering a slightly different variety of product which he prefers. The varieties are different enough so that some of the economies of large-scale production cannot be realized. Each buyer can be considered to have a choice: continue to order his favored variety, or switch over to that of his competitor. Possible payoffs for each course of action are represented in Case I.

Case I

		Buyer B Order Favored Variety		Buyer B Order Competitors Variety	
Buyer A	Order Favored Variety	I	5	II	4
		5		8	
	Order Competitors Variety	III	8	IV	1
		4		1	

In Case I, each player wishes the other would "Order his Competitors Variety." But in the absence of side payments or other inducements, in a single game each has a dominant strategy—order his own favored variety. A single voluntary standard for uniformity probably could not be created, and would not be followed. If the 5-5 outcome seems less than optimal, we could well lay the blame here on the prohibition of side payments. An example of such a single game might be automobile companies, with frequent style changes, purchasing specialized accessories. We could allow a more continual game if we then assume high costs of shifting orders that prevents the cooperation needed to arrive at outcome II say half the time, outcome III the other half.

Case II is also a mixed-motive game, but without a dominant strategy. There is now great incentive for cooperation, since each player prefers outcomes II or III to the old 5-5 solution.

Case II

		Buyer B		
		Order own Variety	Order Competitors Variety
Buyer A	Order Own Variety	5 5	8 7
	Order Competitors Variety	7 8	1 1

Case III is a pure coordination game,

Case III

		Buyer B		
		Order own Variety	Order Competitors Variety
Buyer A	Order Own Variety	5 5	8 8
	Order Competitors Variety	8 8	1 1

In cases such as II or III single standards for uniformity can be very helpful in coordinating purchases allowing a "meeting of minds." This is more apparent when there are a large number of buyers. If they can get together and agree to limit purchases to a few varieties, they all can benefit. Once standards are created, they can be considered as focal points to help coordinate orders.

Appendix B

Standards and the Pipeline Safety Issue: A Case Study

In the mid-1960s the House and Senate Commerce committees held a number of hearings concerning various proposals for federal regulation over the safety of natural gas pipelines. Among other things, a March 4, 1965 pipeline explosion in Natchitoches, Louisiana, which killed seventeen people indicated to many that there was a pressing need in this area. Also important was the action taken by a small group of Pennsylvania engineers, who attempted to prevent pipe from crossing their property until it was made safer. They quickly found, to their dismay, that there was no regulatory body to whom they could appeal. Their efforts did, however, alert the editors of *Chemical Engineering* to the problem.[1]

The response of the natural gas industry to the idea of enforced federal regulations was generally a quite negative one. Typically, they argued that the gas industry had an excellent safety record, and that the type of regulation proposed was completely unwarranted. The Independent Natural Gas Association of America, a group representing the gas *transmission* industry primarily attributed the "excellent" safety record "to our acceptance of, and strict adherence to, the bible of the gas industry—the B31.8 Code for Pressure Piping."[2]

The actual safety performance record of the gas industry is somewhat clouded and obscure. First, there are no definite and accepted standards by which the adequacy of safety can be easily judged. The industry liked to compare its accident-death rate with that from motor vehicles, air transport, railroads, and other people-transport systems. A more appropriate comparison might be with gas and oil tank truck fatalities, but these were not presented at the Hearings. And, of course, this sort of comparison would rarely be conclusive. Second, and more importantly, statistics about distribution line accidents were not available. As Secretary of Transportation Alan Boyd testified:

Safety of distribution lines is a vast unknown. Distribution systems have been in existence for many years and much of the original pipe is still in use even though it is now 30 or 40 years old. There is no readily available information concerning past accidents in distribution systems as there is with transmission pipelines.[3]

An Arthur D. Little study, done at industry request, did estimate that between the years 1957–1966, approximately 46 to 332 people per year were killed due to the natural gas pipeline distribution system.[4]

The principal government witnesses, Alan Boyd and Lee C. White, Federal Power Commission chairman, did not believe that safety in the gas industry was sufficient in terms of the public interest. The federal government was obligated to step in, largely because of the failure of state regulation. In 1966, a large number of states, including Texas, Louisiana, Ohio, Oklahoma, Mississippi, and Illinois, had no safety regulations. These six accounted for 43 per cent of the nation's pipeline mileage. But within a year, spurred by the threat of federal regulation, the National Association of Regulatory and Utility Commissioners (NARUC) succeeded in adding nineteen new states to the list of those with regulations, bringing the total to over forty-six. The states, in essence, merely adopted the ASME-USASI Code B31.8. There was nothing else available. They had insufficient staff, resources, and time to develop their own standards.[5]

The small size of the staff and budget of the states made enforcement of the safety standards totally inadequate. Ralph Nader reported that, for all their duties, five state utility commissions had no engineers, eight had only one, twenty-two had three engineers or less, forty-one had six or less. Only New York and California maintained staffs of any size.[6] A NARUC questionnaire found that only twenty-one out of thirty-five states responding had an inspection staff of its own; and of these twenty-one, twenty had less than five inspectors.

While state enforcement of the regulations was shown to be incredibly meagre, at the Hearings the standard upon which those regulations were based, Code B31.8, also came under severe attack. Perhaps the main weakness was the fact that the code (and thus most state regulations) did not apply to pipe already in the ground. Also the code only recommended, or left to company discretion, such matters as maintenance of pipelines, retesting and marking locations, weld inspection, use of protective coating and cathodic protection, design of compressors and pressure relief valves, and the shipping and handling of pipe.[7] In addition, both British and Swedish regulations provided the public better protection.[8]

The problem was that the code, B31.8, which set the safety standards for the gas industry, seemed to be written by the gas industry itself. The membership of the committee was a major issue in the hearings. The American Society of Mechanical Engineers, sole administrative sponsor for the

USASI activity, cited numbers of organizations represented by engineers on the committee in an attempt to indicate the broad interests represented: the American Insurance Association, American Bureau of Shipping, National Safety Council, Society of Ohio Safety Engineers, U.S. Coast Guard, NARUC, Federal Power Commission, consulting engineers as well as engineers from equipment manufacturers, and the gas industry itself.[9] S. Logan Kerr, however, put numbers beside the various categories of membership, and the story becomes quite different from the one presented by the industry.

Affiliation	B 31.8 oil		B31.8 gas	
	1959	1966	1963	1967
Pipeline Companies	16	25	37	40
Pipe Producers	6	6	12	7
Manufacturers	6	6	6	6
Trade Associations	2	0	1	1
Contractors	0	2	4	2
Research Institutes	0	0	2	2
Testing Laboratories	0	0	1	1
Consultants	0	3	3	2
University Professors	0	0	1	1
Government Agencies	0	2	3	5
	30	44	70	66

The first five categories represent direct industry membership, and the second group of five could be classified as impartial or public interest members. In 1963 the industry-public interest ratio on B31.8 was 6:1. In 1967 industry was still overwhelmingly in control, 56:10. Furthermore, on the 1967 Code Writing Committee for B31.8 the chairman and the two vice-chairmen were from gas or pipelines companies, the secretary was from the trade association.[10] Federal Power Commission chairman Lee C. White contrasted the national electric safety with the natural gas pipeline code: "First the chairman of that group (electric committee) is from the National Bureau of Standards. The representation from Government agencies is far greater than on the B31.8 Committee. Whereas on the B31.8 Committee there are five public agencies, out of approximately 70, on the Electric Code Committee it is 6 among 19."[11]

Amplifying any possible problems caused by the industry-oriented nature of the committee was its seeming secretiveness. The secrecy question was inadequately (or incorrectly) answered by the ASME and USASI at the Hearings. Interested parties claimed that, in accordance with official policy, they were not allowed to see minutes or pertinent committee correspondence, making it very difficult to comment intelligently about the code and proposed or possible modifications.[12] Ralph Nader charged:

> The standards are never issued with revealed technical reasons justifying them. No outsider is allowed to scrutinize the compromises and the facts on which decisions went one way or another. The standards are issued as fiat, authoritarian . . .[13]

The makeup of the committee and the procedural requirement for "consensus" agreement gave industry, or a segment of it, virtual veto power over any changes in the code. Where progress means action the veto power is very comforting to those favoring inaction or the status quo. The standards thus only reflected "accepted" practices of design and construction in the industry.[14] USASI itself stated that "the Piping Code Committee is not a research body; it is not a means for developing new concepts or justifying the use of new and untried materials. These must be developed and proved in industry before they can be adopted . . ." The code committee "cannot lead, but must follow."[15] Somewhat more candidly, a former code committee chairman said that the code:

> . . . cannot include good practices which are not generally accepted. Consequently, new practices that some feel are far superior to old practices cannot get into a code until the industry generally has been convinced that the new practices are acceptable . . .
> . . . standard specification committees tend to be dominated by the manufacturers and the tendency is for tolerances prescribed in a specification to be broad enough as to reduce to a minimum the rejects a manufacturer will have . . .[16]

Though the code committee was industry dominated, though the codes were unenforced and represented only general industry practice, could society nonetheless count on the rational self-interest of business (the "invisible hand") to insure adequate public safety (the social optimal)? The answer is no, due of course to externalities, the divergence of private and social benefits and costs. In general, the companies do not seem to bear the full burden when property is damaged or people are injured. In the Louisiana explosion, for example, seventeen people were killed and five homes destroyed. The company estimated the total property and bodily damage claim at $750,000 (a rather small premium on people's lives), 96 per cent of which was covered by insurance. It should not have been totally surprising therefore to find that in B31.4, the sister code of B31.8 dealing with oil piping, the safety factor was almost twice as great to protect the petroleum industry's personnel and its own property as to protect the public and the property of others.[17]

Given the evidence presented at the Hearings, Congress decided that federal safety regulation of natural gas pipelines was essential. A possibility other than direct regulation, of course, would be to improve the insurance system, and somehow adjust claim payments so that they would more adequately reflect social costs. In other words, internalize those costs presently caused but not borne by the gas companies. (In the Louisiana explosion, Reverend Von Meter, his wife, three daughters, and mother-in-law were killed. It was asserted that the company's economic liability to their survivors was small—there were no survivors.) In this case, since third party (innocent bystander) injuries are not uncommon, society still has to decide *collectively*, though indirectly, on the amount of safety it desires. Direct regulation, however, was more politically feasible, and probably more practical, than this alternative.

Since it was difficult to assess the actual gas safety performance record, a crucial consideration in the governmental decision to intervene in the market was the portent for the future given the rapidly changing industry situation. Growing concentration of population in areas where pipelines were being laid (and had been laid), expanded use of gas, aging and corrosion of lines laid decades previously, and changing technical considerations were continually cited by witnesses.[18] Congress seems to have been convinced that preventive legislation was preferable to the possibility of waiting until additional disasters occurred.

On August 12, 1968 Congress passed the Natural Gas Pipeline Safety Act. Required to promulgate interim safety standards by November, the Department of Transportation's Office of Pipeline Safety naturally chose USASI B31.8, which was adopted for those states without standards. Permanent minimum standards were due by August 1970.[19]

Appendix C

ASME Air Pollution Standards Committee Makeup—1970

This appendix examines the makeup of a particular standards committee. This committee was selected largely because a membership list became available, but also partly for its topical nature and partly because it was represented as an incredibly inclusive committee, "if I understood who these people represent," and that the standards were written "the highest we knew how."[1]

The ASME Air Pollution Standards Committee is a relatively new committee. A very few years ago they published APS-1, which is a standard for ordinances. The object of the committee seems to have been to propose wording for legislation which could be adopted by various states and cities. APS-1 has, in fact, been accepted and passed into law in a number of states. In other areas, such as Boston, the requirements are to be more rigid.

There are twenty-three members of this committee which is chaired by the senior consultant of duPont, an industrial polluter. Four additional engineers represented industrial polluters (Esso, Jones and Laughlin, Proctor and Gamble—2). Four public utility polluters (Union Electric, Indianapolis Power and Light, Public Services Electric, and American Electric Power) are represented. Coal, whose products of combustion pollute the air, is represented by a company and a trade association (Republic Coal, National Coal Association). Equipment manufacturers, whose equipment fires fuel in boilers and the effluents pollute the air, have two representatives (Riley Stoker, Babcock and Wilcox). The manfuacturers of particulate collecting and gaseous removal equipment are represented by one man, E. L. Wilson, former president of the Industrial Gas Cleaning Institute.

TVA, a government polluter, is represented. Also from government are three men in departments responsible for law enforcement (from Illinois, Toronto, and Pennsylvania). Two consultants, active in speaking and publishing in Los Angeles and New York City, are also on the committee. Finally there is the ASME liaison. Virtually all the committee members are experts who have gained some recognition in the pollution field.

It is interesting to note who is not represented. The academic community is not, partly because few professors have done much work in this area. Small business is not well represented for similar reasons. As is often the case, the available expertise tends to reside with the large-scale enterprise. The gas industry, selling a basically clean energy form, will surely be affected by standards imposed on competitors. They are not represented, however, because the very nature of their product has given them little need to study pollution. No gas people are well known in pollution control circles.

Among the fourteen industrial engineers, who could clearly dominate this committee, there is only one with economic incentive to push for tight, tough standards. This is E. L. Wilson from Koppers and the Industrial Gas Cleaning Institute. His position must be difficult, however, in that he would like to be sure not to antagonize customers.

Examining committee membership lists is certainly a far from infallible method for predictions about the standards produced. One perhaps not so obvious reason is that generally most of the committee work is done by six at most, sometimes one, two, or three. The others, busy men, tend to tag along if the standard seems pretty good, adding a little but not much.[2]

The makeup of the ASME Air Pollution Standards Committee, however, does give one every reason to suppose that standards were certainly not written "the highest we knew how." In the objectives to the ASME Pressure Piping Code B.31 (the famed B.31) there is the statement: "While safety is the basic consideration of this code, this factor alone will not necessarily govern the final specifications for any pressure piping system."[3] Very similarly, in this case the tradeoff is basically between cost and the degree of pollution control desired. Given the committee membership, it is not difficult to deduce which receives the greater emphasis.

ASME AIR POLLUTION STANDARDS COMMITTEE 1970

F.T. Bodurtha (Dr.), Chairman
*(Dust, Indirect Heating)

Senior Consultant
E.I. duPont deNemours & Co.
Louviers Building
Wilmington, Delaware 19898
(302-366-3184)

F.E. Gartrell (Dr.),
Vice Chairman

Assistant Director of Health
Division of Health and Safety
Tennessee Valley Authority
715 Edney Building
Chattanooga, Tennessee 37401
(615-755-2593)

*Chairman of Subcommittee

F.W. Church, Secretary

Senior Engineering Associate
Esso Research & Engineering co.
P.O. Box 101
Florham Park, New Jersey 07932
(201-474-6974

G.D. Finster, ASME
Staff Liaison

The American Society of Mechanical Engineers
United Engineering Center
345 East 47th Street
New York, New York 10017
(212-752-6800)

G.H. Damon (Dr.)

Staff Research Coordinator, Explosives
Office of Director of Coal Research
Bureau of Mines, U.S. Dept. of Interior
Washington, D.C. 20240
(202-343-3500)

W.B. Drowley, P.E., Chief

Air Pollution Control Service
Department of Health
One St. Clair Avenue, West
Toronto 7, Ontario, Canada
(416-365-4070, ext. 4081)

W.L. Faith (Dr.)

Consulting Chemical Engineer
2540 Huntington Drive
San Marino, California 91108
(213-287-9383)

L.P. Flood

Consultant
61-62 80th Street
Middle Village
Queens, New York
(212-424-8357)

R.R. French, Chief

Bureau of Air Pollution Control
Illinois Air Pollution Control Board
616 State Office Building
400 S. Spring Street
Springfield, Illinois 62706
(217-525-6580)

W.H. Jaques
*(Sulfur Dioxide Indirect Heating)

Director of Technical Service
Engineering Division
Procter & Gamble Company
ITC Building
Cincinnati, Ohio 45217
(513-562-5065)

W.H. Jukkola (Dr.)

Technical Coordinator
Industrial Wastes Control
Jones & Laughlin Steel Coorporation
3 Gateway Center
Pittsburgh, Pennsylvania 15230
(412-261-7400, ext. 3733)

G.W. Land

Combustion Engineer
Republic Coat & Coke Company
8 South Michigan
Willoughby Tower
Chicago, Illinois 60603
(312-332-3020)

J.F. McLaughlin, Jr.

Executive Assistant
Union Electric Company
P.O. Box 87
St. Louis, Missouri 63166
(314-621-3222)

E.C. Miller
  Alt.–P.F. Seibold
    Mgr., Applied Boiler & Fuel
    Burning, Research Sect.
    Riley Stoker Corp.

Director of Sales Engineering
Riley Stoker Corporation
9 Neponset Street
Worcester, Massachusetts 01601
(617-756-7111)

J.W. Mullan

Assistant Dir., Technical Services Dept.
National Coal Association
1130 17th Street, N.W.
Washington, D.C. 20036
(202-628-4322)

R.H. Pechstein

Assistant Chief Mechanical Engineer
American Electric Power Service Corp.
Two Broadway
New York, New York 10004
(212-422-4800, ext. 692)

A.H. Phelps, Jr.

Procter & Gamble Company
ITC Building
Cincinnati, Ohio 45217
(513-562-6564)

A.C. Stern

School of Public Health
P.O. Box 630
Chapel Hill, North Carolina 27514
(919-966-1370)

V.H. Sussman, Director

Pennsylvania Air Pollution Control Div.
P.O. Box 90
Harrisburg, Pennsylvania 17120
(717-787-6547)

C.B. Vance

Vice President, Power Production
Indianapolis Power & Light Company
25 Monument Circle
(Mail: P.O. Box 1595)
Indianapolis, Indiana 46206
(317-635-6868)

J.B. Walker, Jr.

Manager, Fuel Equipment Design
Power Generation Division
Babcock & Wilcox
Barberton, Ohio 44203
(216-753-4511

E.L. Wilson
  Pres. Industrial Gas
  Cleaning Institute

Mgr., Industrial Gas Cleaning Dept.
Metal Products Division
Koppers Company, Inc.
Scott & McHenry Streets
(Mail: P.O. Box 298)
Baltimore, Maryland 21203
(301-757-2500)

L.A. Winkelman

Manager Plant Engineering
Public Service Electric & Gas Co.
80 Park Place
Newark, New Jersey
(201-622-700, ext. 2859)

Notes

NOTES TO CHAPTER 1
INTRODUCTION

1. Rexmond C. Cochrane, *Measures for Progress* (Washington, D.C.: National Bureau of Standards, 1966), p. 84.
2. *Dictionary of American Biography*, 1935 ed., s.v. "William Sellers."
3. Cochrane, *Measures for Progress*, p. 85.
4. "Take a Number," *Newsweek*, January 17, 1972.
5. H.W. Robb "Significance of Company and National Standards to Industrial Management," in Dickson Reck (ed.), *National Standards in a Modern Economy* (New York: Harper and Row, 1956), p. 296.
6. Robert F. Legget, *Standards in Canada* (Ottawa: Economic Council of Canada, 1970), pp. 56–60; Edward R. Weidlein and Vera Reck, "A Million Years of Standards" in Reck (ed), *National Standards*.
7. Legget, *Standards in Canada*, p. 56.
8. John Perry, *The Story of Standards* (New York· Funk and Wagnalls, 1955), pp. 118–19.
9. Issac Asimov, *Of Space, Time and Other Things* (Garden City, N.Y.: Doubleday, 1965), pp. 16–24.
10. "40-letter, all lower-case alphabet proposed," *Boston Globe*, May 5, 1972, p. 1.
11. Asimov, *Of Space, Time and Other Things*, p. 124.
12. National Bureau of Standards, *A Metric America* (Washington, D.C.: Department of Commerce Special Publication #345, 1971), pp. 15–16.
13. American Standards Association, "Throughout History with Standards," ASA undated publication, p. 1.
14. Perry, *Story of Standards*, p. 5.
15. David K. Lewis, *Convention: A Philosophical Study* (Cambridge: Harvard University Press, 1969).

16. Legget, *Standards in Canada*, p. 39.
17. American Standards Association, "Throughout History with Standards," p. 1.
18. Robert A. Brady, *Organization, Automation and Society* (Berkeley: University of California Press, 1961), p. 142.
19. Marian P. Opala, "The Anatomy of Private Standards-Making Process: The Operating Procedures of the USA Standards Institute," *Oklahoma Law Review* 22 (February, 1969): 45.
20. Baron Whitaker, *Magazine of Standards*, February 1969.
21. *Magazine of Standards*, March 1968.
22. Paul Benner, "The SAE Standards Program," *SAE Journal*, August 1966.
23. Hearings before the Senate Commerce Committee on Motor Vehicle Safety Standards, 90th Cong., 1st Sess. Lowell Bridwell Testimony, March 20, 1967.
24. *ANSI Reporter*, January 5, 1973, p. 1.
25. *U.S.* vs. *Johns-Manville, et al.*, Finding Fact on Application of ASTM, District Court for Eastern Pennsylvania, July 20, 1964.

NOTES TO CHAPTER 2
EARLY AMERICAN AUTOMOBILE STANDARDS:
A CASE STUDY

1. George V. Thompson, "Intercompany Technical Standardization in the Early American Automobile Industry," *Journal of Economic History* 14 (Winter 1954): 3.
2. Ibid., p. 4.
3. Ibid.
4. Ibid., p. 5.
5. John K. Barnes, "The Men Who 'Standardized' Automobile Parts," *The World's Work*, June 1921, p. 206.
6. Thompson, "Intercompany Technical Standardization," p. 6.
7. Ibid., p. 10.
8. Ibid., pp. 8–9.
9. Ibid., pp. 6, 12.
10. Ibid., pp. 13–14.
11. Barnes, "The Men Who 'Standardized' Automobile Parts," p. 206.
12. Ibid.
13. Thompson, "Intercompany Technical Standardization," pp. 15–16. Quote by W.H.T. Tuthell, secretary of Tuthell Spring Company (Chicago) in *SAE Transactions* 6 (1911): 101.
14. Ibid., pp. 16–19.
15. Mancur Olsen, Jr., *The Logic of Collective Action* (Cambridge: Harvard University Press, 1965).
16. Ibid.

NOTES TO CHAPTER 3
SINGLE PRODUCT STANDARDS

1. Norman F. Harriman, *Standards and Standardization* (New York: McGraw-Hill, 1928), p. 114.
2. George Lamb and Carrington Shields, *Trade Association Law and Practice* (Boston: Little, Brown & Co., 1971), p. 75.
3. Department of Commerce, "Simplified Practice: What It Is and What It Offers," 1928.
4. Perry, *Story of Standards*, p. 132.
5. National Industrial Conference Board, *Industrial Standardization* (New York: National Industrial Conference Board, Inc., 1929), p. 77.
6. Harriman, *Standards and Standardization*, p. 114.
7. Perry, *Story of Standards*, p. 132.
8. On World War I, Lamb and Shields, *Trade Association Law and Practice*, p. 75; On World War II, U.S. Department of Labor Studies, "Cost Savings Through Standardization, Simplification and Specialization."
9. William Hard, *Who's Hoover?* (New Jersey: Dodd, Meade & Co., 1928), pp. 200–202.
10. Stuart Chase and F.J. Schlink, *Your Money's Worth* (New York: MacMillan Co., 1927), pp. 175–176.
11. Standards Research Committee, Paper Stationery and Tablet Manufacturers Association, Inc., "Recommended Standards and Specifications for Tablets and Related Products," 1964.
12. U.S. Department of Labor, "Cost Savings Through Standardization, Simplification and Specialization," pp. 16–17.
13. Ibid., p. 18.
14. Ibid., p. 23.
15. Studies by California Consumer Council, Consumers Union, and Dr. Monroe Friedman, cited in Jennifer Cross, *The Supermarket Trap* (Bloomington: Indiana University Press, 1970), pp. 84–86.
16. Hearings before the House Interstate and Foreign Commerce Committee on the Fair Labelling and Packaging Act, 89th Cong., 2nd Sess., Representative Thomas P. O'Neill testimony, p. 22 (1966).
17. Ibid., Ester Peterson Testimony, p. 81.
18. Ibid., Helen Nelson Testimony, California Consumer Council, p. 250.
19. American Can Company, "A History of Packaged Beer and Its Markets in the United States," 1969, p. 10.
20. Cross, *Supermarket Trap*, p. 81.
21. National Bureau of Standards, list of "Product Quantity Standards," May 15, 1971; see also Cross, *Supermarket Trap*, pp. 81–86.
22. Perry, *Story of Standards*, p. 135.
23. See especially the analysis in Lawrence J. White, *The Automobile Industry Since 1945* (Cambridge: Harvard University Press, 1971), Chap. 11.

24. See, for example, Jon E. King, "Antitrust Laws and Standardization," unpublished manuscript, 1972, pp. 35–41.
25. Larry Crabtree, Market Specialist, Tobacco Division, U.S. Department of Agriculture, letter dated August 7, 1972.
26. Fair Labor Standards Act, 29 U.S.C. 201, et seq., 1938.
27. House Hearings on the Fair Labelling and Packaging Act, Harry Schroeter Testimony, VP National Biscuit Company, p. 363.
28. Carolyn Shaw Bell, *Consumer Choice in the American Economy* (New York: Random House, 1967), pp. 250–58.

NOTES TO CHAPTER 4
INTERMEDIATE STANDARDS

1. Jessie V. Coles, *Standards and Labels for Consumers Goods* (New York: Ronald Press, 1949), pp. 246–48; 456–63.
2. Robert F. Legget, *Standards in Canada* (Ottawa: Economic Council of Canada, 1970) pp. 94–95.
3. *Consumer Reports*, October 1972, p. 675.
4. 49 C.F.R. 571.101a, 102.
5. U.S. Department of Labor, "Cost Savings Through Standardization, Simplification and Specialization," section on Industrial Trucks.
6. Charles Lekberg, "The Tyranny of QWERTY," *Saturday Review: Science*, October 1972.
7. American Standards Association, "Throughout History with Standards," ASA undated publication, p. 12.
8. *Consumer Reports*, February 1967, p. 88.
9. Leonard Darvin, Comic Magazine Association of America, letter dated July 6, 1972.

NOTES TO CHAPTER 5
INTERCHANGEABILITY STANDARDS

1. Midge Wilson, Color Association of the United States, Inc., letter dated July 14, 1972.
2. Paul Arnold, "American Standards in Complementary Industries," in Dickson Reck (ed.), *National Standards in a Modern Economy* (New York: Harper and Row, 1956), p. 135
3. Ruth Davis, Center for Computer Sciences and Technology, National Bureau of Standards, lecture at Harvard, April 1972.
4. *International Business Machine Corporation* vs. *U.S.*, 298 U.S. 131 (1936).
5. *Pick Manufacturing Co.* vs. *General Motors*, 80 F 2nd 641 (7th Cir. 1935).
6. *Rupp & Whittengeld Co.* vs. *Elliot*, 131 Fed. 730 (6th Cir. 1904).
7. *Morgan Envelope Co.* vs. *Albany Perforated Paper Co.*, 52 U.S. 425 (1893).
8. *A.B. Dick* vs. *Henry*, 149 Fed. 424 (S.D.N.Y., 1906).
9. *Judson L. Thompson Mfg. Co.* vs. *FTC*, 150 F 2nd 952 (1st Cir. 1945).
10. James M. Ferguson, "Tying Arrangements and Reciprocity: An Economic

Analysis," *Law and Contemporary Problems* 30 (Summer 1965): 552–80.

11. Ward S. Bowman, Jr., "Tying Arrangements and the Leverage Problem," *Yale Law Journal* 67 (November 1957): 19–36; M.L. Burstein, "A Theory of Full-Line Forcing," *Northwestern University Law Review* 55 (March-April 1960): 64–65.

12. W.L. Baldwin and David McFarland, "Tying Arrangements in Law and Economics" *Antitrust Bulletin* 8 (September-December 1963): 743–80; Eugene M. Singer, *Antitrust Economics* (New Jersey: Prentice-Hall, 1968), Chaps. 15, 16.

13. Singer, *Antitrust Economics*, p. 194.

14. Burstein, "Theory of Full-Line Forcing," pp. 67–68.

15. Robert T. Kudrle, "Regulation and Self-Regulation in the Farm Machinery Industry," (unpublished mimeo, University of Minnesota, 1973).

16. Alan Toffler, *Future Shock* (New York: Random House, 1970), Chap. 4.

NOTES TO CHAPTER 6
PRODUCT QUALITY INFORMATION

1. See especially, J. Hirshleifer, "Where Are We in The Theory of Information?", draft, October 31, 1972.

2. Kenneth Boulding, "The Economics of Knowledge and The Knowledge of Economics," *American Economic Review* 56 (May, 1966) reprinted in D.M. Lamberton (ed.), *Economics of Information and Knowledge* (Baltimore: Penguin, 1971), p. 25.

3. Kenneth Arrow, "Economic Welfare and the Allocation of Resources for Invention," 1962, in Lamberton (ed.), *Economics of Information and Knowledge*, p. 141.

4. Ibid, pp. 147–52.

5. Ibid., pp. 141–52.

6. Yoram Barzel, "Optimal Timing of Innovations," *Review of Economics and Statistics* 50 (August 1968); 348–55.

7. Jack Hirshleifer, "The Private and Social Value of Information and the Reward for Innovative Activity," *American Economic Review* 61 (September 1971): 561–74.

8. Arrow, "Economic Welfare and the Allocation of Resources for Invention," in Lamberton (ed.) *Economics of Information and Knowledge*, p. 148.

9. Robert H. Nelson, "The Economics of Honest Trade Practices," draft, 1972, p. 6.

10. Ibid., p. 7.

11. George Akerlof, "The Market for 'Lemons': Quality Uncertainty and the Market Mechanism," *Quarterly Journal of Economics* 84 (August 1970): 488–501.

12. Ibid., p. 488.

13. Carl L. Alsberg, "Economic Aspects of Adulteration and Imitation," *Quarterly Journal of Economics* 46 (November 1931): 8–11.
14. Edward H. Chamberlin, "The Product as an Economic Variable," *Quarterly Journal of Economics* 67 (February 1953): 24–25.
15. See Phillip Nelson, "Information and Consumer Behavior," *Journal of Political Economy* 78 (April 1970): 311–29.
16. Michael R. Darby and Edi Karni, "Free Competition and the Optimal Amount of Fraud," Ohio State University, Division for Economic Research Report 7227, May 1972.
17. George J. Stigler, "The Economics of Information," *Journal of Political Economy* 79 (June 1961): 213–15.
18. Phillip Nelson, "Information and Consumer Behavior."
19. S.A. Ozga, "Imperfect Markets Through Lack of Knowledge," *Quarterly Journal of Economics* 74 (February 1960): 29–52.
20. Robert Nelson, "Economics of Honest Trade Practices."
21. Michael Spence, "Market Signalling," Harvard University Kennedy School Discussion Paper No. 4, February 1972.
22. E. Scott Maynes, "Consumerism: Origin and Research Implications," 1972 discussion paper.
23. Stuart Chase and F.J. Schlink, *Your Money's Worth* (New York: MacMillan Co., 1927), p. 186.
24. Sherman F. Booth, "Quality-Controlled Purchasing," National Bureau of Standards, unpublished article.
25. Wilbur B. England, *Modern Procurement Management: Principles and Cases* (Homewood, Ill.: Richard D. Irwin, 1970), pp. 304–10.
26. National Association of Purchasing Agents, "Standardization Manual: A Book of Principles and Practices for Purchasing Agents," 1964, p. 3.
27. England, *Modern Procurement Management*, p. 312.

NOTES TO CHAPTER 7
QUALITY STANDARDS AND
MARKET STRUCTURE

1. P.G. Agnew, "Standards in Our Social Order," "In the last analysis, not only specifications, but most other standards, except sizes, are essentially definitions." *Industrial Standardization*, June 1940, p. 142.
2. The Aluminum Association, "Aluminum Standards and Data," January 1972.
3. The Aluminum Association, "American National Standard Alloy and Temper Designation Systems for Aluminum," 1971. (originally developed in 1954).
4. National Industrial Conference Board, *Industrial Standardization*, p. 247.
5. E.g., Institute of High Fidelity Standards, in Joan E. Hartman, *Directory of United States Standardization Activities* (Washington: National Bureau of Standards Misc. Publication #288, 1967), p. 126.
6. Association of Home Appliance Manufacturers (AHAM) Standards, HRF 1.
7. E.g., National Association of Building Owners and Managers, in Hartman,

Directory of U.S. Standardization Activities, p. 152. Standard adopted in 1915.

8. E.g., New England Shoe and Leather Association, in Hartman *Directory of U.S. Standardization Activities*, p. 195.

9. *Consumer Reports*, October 1972, pp. 628–37.

10. Michael Hunt, "Competition in the Major Home Appliance Industry: 1960–1970," Ph.D. dissertation, Harvard University, 1972, Chap. 8.

11. Perlite Institute, in Hartman, *Directory of U.S. Standardization Activities* p. 198.

12. Northern Textile Association, in Hartman, *Directory of U.S. Standardization Activities*, p. 198.

13. Air Diffusion Council, "Equipment Test Code 1062R3," 1972.

14. George Otto, Air Diffusion Council, letter dated July 26, 1972.

15. E.g., American Society for Testing and Materials, "Book of ASTM Standards," 1965, Part 21.

16. E.g., Society of the Plastics Industry, in Hartman, *Directory of U.S. Standardization Activities*, p. 213.

17. E.g., Rubber Manufacturers Association, in Hartman, *Directory of U.S. Standardization Activities*, p. 207.

18. Shoe Lace Manufacturers Association (now defunct), "A Manual of Standards," 1966. See John Stewart, Northern Textile Association, letter dated July 7, 1972.

19. National Lime Association, in Hartman, *Directory of U.S. Standardization Activities*, p. 178.

20. E.g., Council for National Cooperation in Aquatics, in Hartman, *Directory of U.S. Standardization Activities*, p. 101.

21. E.g., part of Canadian Welding Code. Canadian Standards Association Standard W47-1969, Welding Qualification Code.

22. Robert H. Nelson, "The Economics of Honest Trade Practices," draft, 1972, p. 6.

23. Bourdon W. Scribner and Russell W. Carr, "Standard for Paper Towels" (Washington: National Bureau of Standards Circular C. 407), cited in Wilbur B. England, *Modern Procurement Management: Principles and Cases* (Homewood, Ill.: Richard D. Irwin, 1970), p. 297.

24. Edwin A. Locke, Jr., President of the American Paper Institute, "United States Involvement in Standardization of Testing Methods," address before the Internation Standards Organization, September 13, 1972. See also John F. Darrow, Senior Vice President of the American Paper Institute, "Paper Standards from a Producer's Point of View," address of TAPP1 annual meeting, February 16, 1972.

25. National Society for the Prevention of Blindness, in Hartman, *Directory of U.S. Standardization Activities*, p. 191.

26. American Society of Mechanical Engineers, Code for the Construction and Inspection of Boilers and Pressure Vessels. See Robert F. Leggett, *Standards in Canada* (Ottawa: Economic Council of Canada, 1970), pp. 75–78. Also see American Standards Association, "Throughout History with Standards," USA undated publication, p. 6.

27. Rexmond C. Cochrane, *Measures for Progress* (Washington, D.C.: National Bureau of Standards, 1966), pp. 121–23.
28. Tibor Scitovsky, "Ignorance as a Source of Oligopoly Power," *American Economic Review* 40 (May 1950); pp. 40–49.
29. Federal Trade Commission, "Preliminary Staff Study on Self Regulation," 1972, p. 10.
30. Manufacturers Standardization Society of the Valve and Fittings Industry, letter dated August 9, 1972.
31. National Commission on Product Safety, Final Report, June 1970, Chap. 4.
32. F.J. Mardulier, "Is There a Future for Voluntary Standardization?", address at ASTM Winter Meeting, January 31, 1967.
33. A.Q. Mowbray, "Show Biz or Hard Facts?" *The Nation*, September 15, 1969.
34. *Magazine of Standards*, November 1966.
35. "Refiners Should Play Ball with S.A.E.," *SAE Journal* , June 1928, p. 673.
36. Ibid.
37. American Petroleum Institute, "Publications and Materials," 1972, p. 51.
38. Wallace N. Seward, American Petroleum Institute, letter dated July 28, 1972.
39. Department of Defense, in Hartman, *Directory of U.S. Standardization Activities*, p. 246.
40. Hearings before the House Small Business Committee on the Effect upon Small Business of Voluntary Industrial Standards, 90th Cong. 1st. Sess., J. Herbert Holloman Testimony, June 1, 1967.
41. H.W. Emmons, Vice President, American Society of Mechanical Engineers, interview held Spring 1970.
42. E.g., American National Standards Institute, "What is the ANSI?", p. 9.
43. National Industrial Conference Board, *Industrial Standardization*, p. 260.
44. Leonard Darvin, Code Authority Comics Magazine Association of America, letter dated July 6, 1972.
45. Code of the Comics Magazine Association of America, 1971.
46. Quoted in Hunt, "Competition in the Major Home Appliance Industry," p. 243.
47. Ibid, Chap. 8.
48. Lol C. Verman, *Standardization: A New Discipline* (Hamden, Conn.: Shoe String Press, 1973), p. 272.
49. Charles Sharpston, "Standardization" (New York: United Nations Industrial Development Organization Monograph #12, 1967), p. 20.
50. Ibid.
51. National Industrial Conference Board, *Industrial Standardization*, p. 213.
52. Ibid., p. 93.
53. Ibid.
54. Ibid., pp. 81–83.
55. Nelson C. Brown, *Lumber* (New York: Wiley, 1947), pp. 177, 251; Stanley F. Horn, *This Fascinating Lumber Business* (Indianapolis: Bobbs-Merrill, 1951), p. 211; Samuel P. Kaidanovsky, "Consumer Standards" (Washington: Temporary National Economic Commission

Investigation of Economic Power, Monograph #24, 1941), p. 201.

56. L.W. Smith and L.W. Wood, *History of Yard Lumber Size Standards* (Washington D.C.: Forest Products Laboratory, Forest Service, Department of Agriculture, 1964), pp. 2–6.

57. "Recommendations as to Standard Sizes and Grades of Lumber are Explained by the Central Committee," *American Lumberman*, December 1, 1923, p. 45.

58. Ibid.

59. Summary of speeches by Dr. Wilson Compton, National Lumber Manufacturers Association, in *American Lumberman*, July 15 and July 29, 1922, by Smith and Wood, "History of Yard Lumber Size Standards," p. 8.

60. Horn, *This Fascinating Lumber Business*, p. 211.

61. Smith and Wood, "History of Yard Lumber Size Standards,", p. 24.

62. Thomas C. Schelling, *The Strategy of Conflict*, (New York: Oxford U. Press, Galaxy, 1963), Chap. 3. (The argument, of course, is not stated in precisely these terms.)

63. Smith and Wood, "History of Yard Lumber Size Standards," p. 24.

64. Hearings before the House Small Business Committee on New Softwood Lumber Standards, 91st Cong., 2nd Sess., p. 141 (1970).

65. Cochrane, *Measures for Progress*, p. 38.

66. National Bureau of Standards, Annual Report, 1906, p. 15.

67. Marian P. Opala, "The Anatomy of Private Standards-Making Process: The Operating Procedures of the USA Standards Institute," *Oklahoma Law Review* 22 (February 1969): 64, 68.

68. H.G. Rickover, "Who Protects the Public?" *Materials Evaluation*, December 1968.

69. Hunt, "Competition in the Major Home Appliance Industry," Chap. 8.

70. Kudrle, "Regulation and Self-Regulation in the Farm Machinery Industry," p. 7.

71. E.g., Donald A. Turner, "Consumer Protection by Private Joint Action," address at the N.Y. State Bar Association Law Symposium, 1967, p. 42.

72. "The Birth of Cooperative Research," *SAE Journal*, February 1955, p. 63; "Cooperative Fuel Research and Its Results," *SAE Journal*, August 1929, p. 171.

73. Frank E. Hodgdon, American Gas Association Laboratories, letter dated August 14, 1972.

74. American Gas Association, comments in response to a Federal Trade Commission inquiry with respect to private testing and certification programs, 1972, p. 1.

75. Ibid., Appendix A; also Frank Hodgdon letter.

76. Hartman, *Directory of U.S. Standardization Activities*, p. 11; see also Aluminum Association, "Aluminum Standards and Data."

77. F.M. Scherer, *Industrial Market Structure and Economic Performance* (Chicago: Rand McNally, 1970), p. 159.

78. "Steel Gets His with the Big One," *Business Week*, April 11, 1964, pp. 27–28.

79. Samuel M. Loescher, *Imperfect Collusion in the Cement Industry* (Cambridge: Harvard University Press, 1959), p. 159.
80. E.g., *Milk and Ice Cream Can Institute* vs. *FTC*, 152 F 2d 478, 480 (9th Cir. 1946); *Bond Crown and Cork Company* vs. *FTC*, 176 F 2d 974 (4th Cir. 1949); *C-O-Two Fire Equipment Co.* vs. *United States*, 197 F 2d 489 (9th Cir. 1952) *Cert. denied*, 344 U.S. 892 (1952).
81. *Standard Sanitary Manufacturing Co.* vs. *United States* 226 U.S. 20 (1912).
82. *United States* vs. *Institute of Carpet Manufacturers* 1940-43 Trade Cases, 56, 097 (S.D.N.Y. 1941).
83. *United States* vs. *Trenton Potteries Co.* 273 U.S. 392, 398 (1927).
84. Hearings before the House Small Business Committee on the Effect Upon Small Business of Voluntary Industrial Standards, 90th Cong., 1st Sess., pt. 1 at 90-98 (1967).
85. Ibid., in *Report* of these hearings, p. 47.
86. Ibid., pp. 74–75.
87. Hearings before the House Small Business Committee on the Rural and Urban Problems of Small Businessmen, 91st Cong., 2nd Sess., pp. 47–53 (1970).
88. Allen D. Manvel, "Local Land and Building Regulation," prepared for the consideration of the National Commission on Urban Problems, Report #6, 1968, pp. 12, 33, 34.
89. Organization for European Economic Cooperation, "Some Aspects of Standardization in the United States and Europe," 1953, pp. 61–62. See Also C.S. McCamy, "A Half-Century of Photographic Standardization," National Bureau of Standards, 1967.
90. "Technology and World Trade" (Washington, D.C.: National Bureau of Standards Misc. Publication 284, 1967), p. 48.
91. Leggett, *Standards in Canada* p. 261; W.E. Andrus, Office of Engineering and Information Processing Standards, National Bureau of Standards, interview held August 1972.
92. E.g., Industrial Fasteners Institute, *Fasteners,* Winter 1967, pp. 8–9.
93. *Application of American Society for Testing and Materials*, 231 F. Supp. 686. (E.D. Pa 1964); *United States* vs. *Johns-Manville Corp.*, 1966 Trade Cases par. 71.961 (E.D. Pa 1966); *United States* vs. *Johns-Manville Corp.*, 1967 Trade Cases par. 72.184 (E.D. Pa 1967).
94. John F. Graybeal, "Product Safety: Law and Administration," National Commission on Product Safety, Supplemental Studies, Vol. III; Federal Trade Commission, "Preliminary Staff Study of Self-Regulation"; H. Richard Wachtel, "Products Standards and Certification Programs," *Antitrust Bulletin* 13 (Spring 1968); Jon E. King, "Antitrust Law and Standardization," unpublished manuscript, 1972.
95. Some addition antitrust sources: Richard McLaren, "Voluntary Product Standards and the Antitrust Law," *Magazine of Standards*, October 1969; American National Standards Institute, "Antitrust Implications of Metric Conversion," 1971; Allen I. Sachs, "Voluntary Standards and the Antitrust Laws," unpublished manuscript, 1970.

Some addition international sources: United Nations, "International Standardization in Developing Countries," 1964; Boris Kit, "Economic Impact of International Standardization on United States Industry and Trade," National Bureau of Standards, unpublished paper, 1966; American National Standards Institute, "International Standards: Impact on U.S. Business," 1972.

NOTES TO CHAPTER 8
STANDARDS CREATION
IN THE UNITED STATES

1. Report of the Panel on Engineering and Commodity Standards of the Department of Commerce Technical Advisory Board, February 2, 1965. (Hereafter cited as *The LaQue Report.*)
2. Ibid.
3. National Industrial Conference Board, *Trade Associations* (New York: National Industrial Conference Board, Inc., 1925), pp. 18–25; Joseph F. Bradley, *The Role of Trade Associations and Professional Business Societies in America* (University Park, Pa.: Pennsylvania State U. Press, 1965), pp. 1–4; George Lamb and Carrington Shields, *Trade Association Law and Practice* (Boston: Little, Brown, 1971).
4. *Consumer Reports*, October 1972, p. 675.
5. Frank E. Hodgdon, American Gas Association Laboratories, letter dated August 14, 1972.
6. Code of the Comics Magazine Association of America, 1971.
7. Congressional Record, October 20, 1966 (remarks by Congressman John D. Dingall).
8. Michael Hunt, "Competition in the Major Home Appliance Industry: 1960–1970," Ph.D. dissertation, Harvard University, 1972, Chap. 8.
9. William Harris, "Impact of Professional Societies," in Boyd Keenan (ed.), *Science and the University* (New York: Columbia University Press, 1966); *International Encyclopedia of the Social Sciences*, 1968 ed., s.v. "Engineering" by William Evan.
10. Membership numbers exclude student members, from Engineers Joint Council, "Directory of Engineering Societies," 1970. Engineering societies have received little academic attention, so much of the discussion in this book derives from responses to the author's detailed questionnaires, plus more than a dozen personal interviews, primarily with national officers, conducted in the Spring of 1970.
11. M.I.T. Professor Rogowski, ASME and SAE member, interview held Spring 1970. Says Rogowski of the SAE local: "Very rarely do we get good technical papers in Boston."
12. M.I.T. Professor Biggs, ASCE member; Harvard Professor Emmons, ASME Vice President. Interviews Spring 1970.
13. *International Encyclopedia of the Social Sciences*, 1968 ed., s.v. "Engineering"; Harvard Professor Mimno (ret) a principal IEEE standards official, said the IEEE is an educational institution as Harvard is. He sees the ASME as more of a trade association.

14. C. Richard Soderberg, "The American Engineer," in Kenneth S. Lynn (ed.,), *The Professions in America* (Boston: Houghton Mifflin, 1965).
15. William Kornhauser, *Scientists in Industry* (Berkeley: University of California Press, 1962), p. 88.
16. William E. Reaser, *American Society of Mechanical Engineers*, letter dated March 6, 1970.
17. Earle C. Miller, Vice President Region I, ASME, letters to the New England governors, February 3, 1970. See also ASME "Council Policy: Guide to Society Legislative Activities."
18. M.I.T. Professor Biggs, ASCE member; Northeastern Professor Spencer, local ASCE officer. Interviews held Spring 1970.
19. Harvard Professor Mimno (ret), IEEE standards official, interview held Spring 1970.
20. C.G. Veinott, "Standardization: A Stated Objective of the Institute," *Electrical Engineering*, October 1961.
21. William Evan, "Role Strain and the Norm of Reciprocity in Research Organizations," *American Journal of Sociology* 68 (November 1962); 346–54.
22. Soderberg, "The American Engineer."
23. Kornhauser, *Scientists in Industry*, reports that a survey of seventy-three member companies of the National Industrial Conference Board shows that fifty-six pay the dues for society membership.
24. G.W. McCullough speech summarized in "Relationship between Engineering Societies and Industry," an Engineering Joint Council Symposium, January 18–19, 1965.
25. "SAE in Profile," society literature; Paul Benner, "The SAE Standards Program," *SAE Journal*, August 1966.
26. *Mechanical Engineering*, January 1970. IEEE income statistics for 1968 show 43 per cent of income coming from membership dues, 11 per cent from advertising, 21 per cent from sale of publications. H.L. Nicol, IEEE, letter dated April 17, 1970.
27. National Industrial Conference Board, *Industrial Standardization*, p. 63.
28. George Taylor, AFL-CIO, letter dated April 15, 1970.
29. Emmons interview; F.J. Mardulier, "ASTM: Its Function and Philosophy" author's copy.
30. "ASTM and the Voluntary Standardization System," society literature, 1969; Robert Legget, *Standards in Canada* (Ottawa: Economic Council of Canada, 1970), pp. 125–27; Joan E. Hartman, *Directory of United States Standardization Activities* (Washington: National Bureau of Standards Misc. Publication #288, 1967), pp. 57–62.
31. *Materials Research and Standards*, July 1968.
32. *U.S.* vs. *Johns-Manville et al.*, Finding of Fact on Application of ASTM, District Court for Eastern Pennsylvania, July 20, 1964.
33. "NFPA," society literature, 1972; Hartman, *Directory of U.S. Standardization Activities*, p. 171.

34. Underwriters' Laboratories, Inc., "Testing for Public Safety," society literature; Hartman, *Directory of U.S. Standardization Activities*, pp. 229–31.
35. National Commission on Product Safety, Final Report, pp. 55–57; Ralph Nader, *Beware!* (New York: Law-Arts Paper, 1971), pp. 66–69.
36. E.g. J. Gaillard, *Industrial Standardization: Its Principles and Applications* (New York: H.W. Wilson Co., 1934) p. 119.
37. American National Standards Institute, Progress Report, 1971. Hearings before the House Small Business Committee on the Effect upon Small Business of Voluntary Industrial Standards, pp. 386–87.
38. Harold Walker, ANSI, interview held August 1972.
39. This situation is acknowledged by ANSI. See "What Is ANSI?", society literature.
40. National Commission on Product Safety, Final Report, p. 52.
41. Warren Magnuson and Jean Casper, *The Dark Side of the Marketplace* (Englewood Cliffs, N.J.: Prentice-Hall, 1968), Chap. 5; Morris Kaplan, Consumers Union, letter dated March 5, 1970.
42. James Ridgeway, "Standards to Protect the Buying Public," *The New Republic*, May 1, 1965, pp. 9–10.
43. Marian P. Opala, "The Anatomy of Private Standards-Making Process: The Operating Procedures of the USA Standards Institute," *Oklahoma Law Review* 22 (February 1969): 45–68.
44. National Bureau of Standards, Annual Report, 1971, also W.E. Andrus, Office of Engineering and Information Standards, National Bureau of Standards, interview held August 1972.
45. Hearings before the House Small Business Committee on the Effect upon Small Business of Voluntary Industrial Standards, p. 16.
46. Opala, "The Anatomy of Private Standards-Making Process," pp. 32–33.
47. W.A. Philo, Engineering Standards Services, National Bureau of Standards, interview held August, 1972; also *LaQue Report*.
48. Hearings before the House Small Business Committee on the Effect upon Small Business of Voluntary Industrial Standards, p. 6. (The "criteria" are condensed for the sake of brevity.)

NOTES TO CHAPTER 9
SUMMARY AND CONCLUSIONS

1. George Akerlof, "The Market for 'Lemons': Quality Uncertainty and the Market Mechanism," *Quarterly Journal of Economics* 84 (August 1970): 488–501.
2. Mancur Olsen, Jr., *The Logic of Collective Action* (Cambridge: Harvard University Press, 1965).

NOTES TO APPENDIX B
STANDARDS AND THE PIPELINE
SAFETY ISSUE: A CASE STUDY

1. Fredrick C. Price, "Long Distance Pipelines: Shouldn't They Be Safer?" *Chemical Engineering*, November 22, 1965. See also Fredrick C. Price, "Safety of Long Distance Pipelines," speech at the annual meeting of the Fire Marshals Association of America, May 16, 1966.
2. Hearings before the House Interstate and Foreign Commerce Committee on Natural Gas Pipeline Safety, 90th Cong. 1st and 2nd Sess., W.A. Strauss (INGAA) testimony, February 28, 1968.
3. Hearings before the House Interstate and Foreign Commerce Committee on Natural Gas Pipeline Safety, 90th Cong. 1st and 2nd Sess., W.A. Strauss (INGAA) testimony, February 28, 1968.
3. Hearings before the Senate Commerce Committee on Natural Gas Pipeline Safety Regulations, 90th Cong., 1st Sess., April 19, 1967 (hereafter cited as *The Gas Hearings*).
4. *The Gas Hearings*, testimony of H.D. Borger, Consolidated Natural Gas Systems.
5. Ibid., testimony of Alan Boyd (Department of Transportation), Lee C. White (Federal Power Commission), Andrew Biemiller, (AFL-CIO), and Frederick Allen, (NARUC).
6. Ibid., testimony of Ralph Nader.
7. Ibid., testimony of Boyd and White.
8. Ibid., testimony of S. Logan Kerr, consulting engineer.
9. Ibid., testimony of Frank Williams (ASME), and Borger.
10. Ibid., testimony of Kerr.
11. Ibid., testimony of White
12. Ibid., testimony of Kerr; Hearings before the Senate Commerce Committee on the Safety of Interstate Natural Gas Pipelines, 89th Cong., 2nd Sess. testimony of Fredrick Lang, S.E. Pennsylvania Landowners Association, Aug. 29, 1966.
13. *The Gas Hearings* testimony of Nader.
14. Ibid., testimony of Boyd, White, Nader.
15. Ibid, testimony of Francis McCune, USASI.
16. Fred A. Hough, "The New Gas Transmission and Distribution Piping Code," *Gas Magazine*, January 1955, quoted at *The Gas Hearings* by White.
17. *The Gas Hearings*, testimony of Senator Vance Hartke.
18. Hearings before the Senate Commerce Committee on the Safety of Interstate Natural Gas Pipelines, testimony of Lang; also *The Gas Hearings*, testimony of Boyd, White.
19. Hearings before the Senate Commerce Committee on Gas Pipeline Safety Oversight. 91st, Cong. 1st, Sess. July 9, 1969.

NOTES TO APPENDIX C
ASME AIR POLLUTION STANDARDS
COMMITTEE MAKEUP—1970

1. Earle C. Miller, ASME Vice President, interviews held Spring, 1970.
2. Much of the discussion in the last three paragraphs is based on correspondence with Henry H. Hemenway, formerly of Riley Stoker and Western Precipitation Corps.
3. Ibid., Dr. M.N. Clair, Thompson & Lichtner, past national officer ASCE, ASTM, interview held Spring, 1970.

References

BOOKS

Asimov, Issac. *Of Space, Time and Other Things.* Garden City, New York: Doubleday, 1965.

Bell, Carolyn Shaw. *Consumer Choice in the American Economy.* New York: Random House, 1967.

Bradley, Joseph F. *The Role of Trade Associations and Professional Business Societies in America.* University Park, Pa.: Pennsylvania State University Press, 1965.

Brady, Robert A. *Organization, Automation and Society.* Berkeley: University of California Press, 1961.

Brown, Nelson C. *Lumber.* New York: Wiley, 1947.

Chase, Stuart and Schlink, F. J. *Your Money's Worth.* New York: MacMillan, 1927.

Cochrane, Rexmond C. *Measures for Progress.* Washington, D.C.: National Bureau of Standards, 1966.

Coles, Jessie V. *Standards and Labels for Consumers Goods.* New York: Ronald Press, 1949.

Cross, Jennifer. *The Supermarket Trap.* Bloomington: Indiana University Press, 1970.

England, Wilbur B. *Modern Procurement Management: Principles and Cases.* Homewood, Illinois: Richard D. Irwin, 1970.

Gaillard, J. *Industrial Standardization: Its Principles and Applications.* New York: H. W. Willson, 1934.

Hard, William. *Who's Hoover?* New Jersey: Dodd, Meade & Co., 1928.

Harriman, Norman F. *Standards and Standardization.* New York: McGraw-Hill, 1928.

Hartman, Joan E. *Directory of United States Standardization Activities.* Washington, D.C.: National Bureau of Standards, 1967.

Horn, Stanley F. *This Fascinating Lumber Business.* Indianapolis: Bobbs-Merrill. 1951.

Keenan, Boyd, ed. *Science and the University*. New York: Columbia University Press, 1966.

Kornhauser, William. *Scientists in Industry*. Berkeley: University of California Press, 1962.

Lamb, George and Shields, Carrington. *Trade Association Law and Practice*. Boston: Little, Brown & Co., 1971.

Legget, Robert F. *Standards in Canada*, Ottawa: Economic Council of Canada, 1970.

Lewis, David K. *Convention: A Philosophical Study*. Cambridge: Harvard University Press, 1969.

Loescher, Samuel M. *Imperfect Collusion in the Cement Industry*. Cambridge: Harvard University Press, 1959.

Lynn, Kenneth S., ed. *The Professions in America*. Boston: Houghton Mifflin, 1965.

Magnuson, Warren and Carper, Jean. *The Dark Side of the Marketplace*. Englewood Cliffs, N.J.: Prentice-Hall, 1968.

Nader, Ralph. *Beware!* New York: Law-Arts Paper, 1971.

National Industrial Conference Board. *Industrial Standardization*. New York: National Industrial Conference Board, Inc. 1929.

——. *Trade Associations*. New York: National Industrial Conference Board, Inc., 1925.

Olsen, Mancur, Jr. *The Logic of Collective Action*. Cambridge: University Press, 1965.

Perry, John. *The Story of Standards*. New York: Funk and Wagnalls, 1955.

Reck, Dickson, ed. *National Standards in a Modern Economy*. New York: Harper and Row, 1956.

Schelling, Thomas C. *The Strategy of Conflict*. New York: Oxford University Press, Galaxy, 1963.

Scherer, F. M. *Industrial Market Structure and Economic Performance*. Chicago: Rand McNally, 1970.

Singer, Eugene M. *Antitrust Economics*. New Jersey: Prentice-Hall, 1968.

Toffler, Alan. *Future Shock*. New York: Random House, 1970.

Verman, Lol C. *Standardization: A New Discipline*. Hamden, Conn.: Shoe String Press, 1973.

White, Lawrence J. *The Automobile Industry Since 1945*. Cambridge: Harvard University Press, 1971.

ARTICLES AND MANUSCRIPTS

Akerlof, George, "The Market for 'Lemons': Quality Uncertainty and the Market Mechanism." *Quarterly Journal of Economics* 84 (August 1970).

Alsberg, Carl L. "Economic Aspects of Adulteration and Imitation." *Quarterly Journal of Economics* 44 (November 1931).

Arrow, Kenneth. "Economic Welfare and the Allocation of Resources for Invention." In D. M. Lamberton, ed., *Economics of Information and Knowledge*. Baltimore: Penguin, 1971.

Baldwin, W. L. and McFarland, David. "Tying Arrangements in Law and Economics." *Antitrust Bulletin* 8 (September 1963).

Barzel, Yoram. "Optimal Timing of Innovations." *Review of Economics and Statistics* 50 (August 1968).

Boulding, Kenneth. "The Economics of Knowledge and the Knowledge of Economics." *American Economic Review* 56 (May 1966).

Bowman, Ward S., Jr. "Tying Arrangements and the Leverage Problem." *Yale Law Journal* 67 (November 1957).

Burstein, M. L. "A Theory of Full-Line Forcing," *Northwestern University Law Review* 55 (March 1960).

Chamberlin, Edward H. "The Product as an Economic Variable," *Quarterly Journal of Economics* 67 (February 1953).

Darby, Michael R. and Karni, Edi. "Free Competition and the Optimal Amount of Fraud," Ohio State University. Division for Economic Research Report 7227, May 1972.

Evan, William. "Role Strain and the Norm of Reciprocity in Research Organizations." *American Journal of Sociology* 68 (November 1962).

Ferguson, James M. "Tying Arrangements and Reciprocity: An Economic Analysis." *Law and Contemporary Problems* 30 (Summer 1965).

Hirshleifer, Jack. "The Private and Social Value of Information and the Reward for Innovative Activity." *American Economic Review* 61 (September 1971).

———. "Where Are We in the Theory of Information?" Draft, October 31, 1972.

Hunt, Michael. "Competition in the Major Home Appliance Industry: 1960–1970." Ph.D. dissertation, Harvard University, 1972.

King, Jon E. "Antitrust Laws and Standardization," Unpublished manuscript, 1972.

Kudrle, Robert T. "Regulation and Self-Regulation in the Farm Machinery Industry." University of Minnesota, unpublished mimeo, 1973.

Maynes, E. Scott. "Consumerism: Origin and Research Implication." Discussion paper, 1972.

Nelson, Phillip. "Information and Consumer Behavior." *Journal of Political Economy* 78 (April 1970).

Nelson, Robert H. "The Economics of Honest Trade Practices." Draft, 1972.

Opala, Marian P. "The Anatomy of Private Standards-Making Process: The Operating Procedures of the USA Standards Institute." *Oklahoma Law Review* 22 (February 1969).

Ozga, S. A. "Imperfect Markets Through Lack of Knowledge," *Quarterly Journal of Economics* 74 (February 1960).

Sachs, Allen I. "Voluntary Standards and the Antitrust Laws." Unpublished manuscript, 1970.

Scitovsky, Tibor. "Ignorance as a Source of Oligopoly Power." *American Economic Review* 40 (May 1950).

Spence, Michael. "Marketing Signalling." Harvard University Kennedy School Discussion Paper #4, February 1972.

Stigler, George J. "The Economics of Information," *Journal of Political Economy* 79 (June 1961).

Thompson, George V. "Intercompany Technical Standardization in the Early American Automobile Industry." *Journal of Economic History* 14 (Winter 1954).

Wachtel, H. Richard. "Production Standards and Certification Programs." *Antitrust Bulletin* 13 (Spring 1968).

ANTITRUST CASES

A. B. Dick v. *Henry*, 149 Fed 424 (S.D.N.Y., 1906).

Bond Crown and Cork Company v. *FTC*, 176 F 2d 974 (4th Cir 1949).

C-O-Two Fire Equipment Co. v. *U.S.*, 197 F 2d 489 (9th Cir 1952).

Institute of Carpet Manufacturers; U.S. v. 1940–43 Trade Cases 56, 097 (S.D.N.Y. 1941).

International Business Machine Corporation v. *U.S.*, 298 131 (1936).

Johns-Manville Corp.; U.S. v. Finding of Fact on Application of ASTM, 231 F. Supp. 686 (E.D. Pa. 1964). 1966 Trade Cases par 71.961 (E.D. Pa 1966). 1967 Trade Cases par 72. 184 (E.D. Pa. 1967).

Judson L. Thompson Manufacturing Co. v. *FTC*, 150 F 2nd 952 (1st Cir 1945).

Milk and Ice Cream Can Institute v. *FTC*, 152 F 2d 478 (9th Cir 1946).

Morgan Envelope Co. v. *Albany Perforated Paper Co.*, 52 US 425 (1893).

Pick Manufacturing Co. v. *General Motors Corp.*, 80 F 2nd 641 (7th Cir 1935).

Rupp and Wittengeld Co. v. *Elliot*, 131 Fed 730 (6th Cir 1904).

Standard Sanitary Manufacturing Co. v. *U.S.*, 226 US 20 (1912).

Trenton Potteries Co.; US v. 273 US 392 (1927).

GOVERNMENT SOURCES

Organization for European Economic Cooperation. *Some Aspects of Standardization in the United States and Europe*, 1953.

United Nations. *International Standardization in Developing Countries*, 1964.

United Nations. *Standardization* by Charles Sharpston. United Nations Industrial Development Organization Monograph No. 12, 1967.

U.S. Congress, House Committee on Interstate and Foreign Commerce. *Fair Labelling and Packaging Act*, 89th Cong., 2nd Sess., 1966.

U.S. Congress, House Committee on Interstate and Foreign Commerce. *Natural Gas Pipeline Safety*, 90th Cong., 2nd Sess., 1968.

U.S. Congress, House Committee on Small Business. *Effect upon Small Business of Voluntary Industrial Standards*, 90th Cong., 1st Sess., 1967.

U.S. Congress, House Committee on Small Business. *New Softwood Lumber Standards*, 91st Cong., 2nd Sess., 1970.

U.S. Congress, House Committee on Small Business. *Rural and Urban Problems of Small Businessmen*, 91st Cong., 2nd Sess., 1970.

U.S. Congress, Senate Committee on Commerce. *Gas Pipeline Safety Oversight*, 91st Cong., 1st Sess., 1969.

U.S. Congress, Senate Committee on Commerce. *Motor Vehicle Safety Standards*, 90th Cong., 1st Sess. 1967.

U.S. Congress, Senate Committee on Commerce. *Natural Gas Pipeline Safety Regulations*, 90th Cong., 1st Sess., 1967.

U.S. Congress, Senate Committee on Commerce. *Safety of Interstate Natural Gas Pipelines*, 89th Cong., 2nd Sess., 1966.

U.S. Department of Agriculture. Forest Service, Forest Products Laboratory. *History of Yard Lumber Size Standards* by L. W. Smith and L. W. Wood, 1966.

U.S. Department of Agriculture. Tobacco Division. Larry Crabtree, letter dated August 7, 1972.

U.S. Department of Commerce. National Bureau of Standards. *A Half-Century of Photographic Standardization* by C. S. McCamy, 1967.

U.S. Department of Commerce. National Bureau of Standards. *A Metric America*. Special Publication No. 345. 1971.

U.S. Department of Commerce. National Bureau of Standards. *Annual Report* 1906, 1971.

U.S. Department of Commerce. National Bureau of Standards. *Economic Impact of International Standardization on United States Industry and Trade* by Boris Kit, 1966 (unpublished).

U.S. Department of Commerce. National Bureau of Standards. Ruth Davis, lecture at Harvard, April 1972.

U.S. Department of Commerce. National Bureau of Standards. Interviews with W. E. Andrus, Office of Engineering Standards Services; also Mr. Vadelund, runs Fair Packaging and Labelling Act, and Dr. Crane, economist. August 1972.

U.S. Department of Commerce. National Bureau of Standards. *Quality-Controlled Purchasing* by Sherman F. Booth (unpublished).

U.S. Department of Commerce. National Bureau of Standards. *Technology and World Trade*. Misc. Publication No. 284. 1967.

U.S. Department of Commerce. *Report of the Panel on Engineering and Commodity Standards of the Department of Commerce and Technical Advisory Board* (The "LaQue Report") 1965.

U.S. Department of Commerce. *Simplified Practice: What It is and What It Offers*. 1928.

U.S. Department of Labor. *Cost Savings Through Standardization, Simplification and Specialization*.

U.S. Federal Trade Commission. *Preliminary Staff Study on Self Regulation* 1972.

U.S. National Commission on Product Safety. *Final Report to the President and Congress*, June 1970, with Supplemental Studies.

U.S. National Commission on Urban Problems. Allen D. Manvel, "Local Land and Building Regulation," Report No. 6, 1968.

U.S. Temporary National Economic Commission. Investigation of Economic Power. *Consumer Standards* by Samuel P. Kaidanovsky. Monograph No. 24. 1941.

MAGAZINES AND DICTIONARIES

Agnew, P.G. "Standards in our Social Order," *Industrial Standardization*, June 1940.

Barnes, John K. "The Men Who 'Standardized' Automobile Parts." *World's Work*, June 1921.

Benner, Paul. "The SAE Standards Program," *SAE Jorrnal*. August 1966.

Dictionary of American Biography, 1935 ed., s.v. "William Sellers."

Hough, Fred A. "The New Gas Transmission and Distribution Piping Code." *Gas Magazine*, January 1955.

Inernational Encyclopedia of the Social Sciences, 1968 ed., s.v. "Engineering." by William Evan.

Lekberg, Charles. "The Tyranny of QWERTY." *Saturday Review: Science*, October 1972.

Mowbray, A. Q. "Show Biz or Hard Facts?" *Nation*, September 15, 1969.

Price, Fredrick C. "Long Distance Pipelines: Shouldn't They Be Safer?" *Chemical Engineering*, November 22, 1965.

Rickover, H. G. "Who Protects the Public?" *Materials Evaluation*, December 1968.

Veinott, C. G. "Standardization: A Stated Objective of the Institute." *Electrical Engineering*, October 1961

OTHER MAGAZINE AND NEWSPAPER ARTICLES

American Lumberman. "Recommendations as to Standard Sizes and Grades of Lumber are Explained by the Central Committee," December 1, 1923.

ANSI Reporter, January 5, 1973.

Boston Globe. "40 letter, all lower-case alphabet proposed," May 5, 1972.

Business Week. "Steel Gets Hit with the Big One," April 11, 1964.

Consumer Reports, February 1967, October 1972.

Fasteners, Winter 1967.

Magazine of Standards, November 1966, March 1968, February 1969, October 1969.

Materials Research and Standards, July 1968.

Mechanical Engineering, January 1970.

Newsweek. "Take a Number," January 17, 1972.

SAE Journal. "Birth of Cooperative Research," February 1955; "Cooperative Fuel Research and Its Results," August 1929; "Refiners Should Play Ball with SAE," June 1928.

ASSOCIATION AND SOCIETY SOURCES

Air Diffusion Council. Equipment Test Code 1062R3, 1972.

———. George Otto, letter dated July 26, 1972.

Aluminum Association. "American National Standard Alloy and Temper Designation Systems for Aluminum." 1971.

———. "Aluminum Standards and Data," January 1972.

American Can Company. "A History of Packaged Beer and Its Markets in the United States," 1969.

American Federation of Labor and Congress of Industrial Organizations. George Taylor, letter dated April 15, 1970.

American Gas Association. "Comments in Response to a Federal Trade Commission Inquiry with Respect to Private Testing and Certification Programs," 1972.

——. Frank Hodgdon, letter dated August 14, 1972.

American National Standards Institute. "Antitrust Implications of Metric Conversion," 1971.

——. "International Standards: Impact on U.S. Business," 1972.

——. Progress Report, 1971.

——. Harold Walker, Interview held August 1972.

——. "What Is ANSI?"

——. (American Standards Association). "Throughout History with Standards."

American Paper Institute. John Darrow, "Paper Standards from a Producer's Point of View." Address at TAPPI annual meeting, February 16, 1972.

——. Edwin A. Locke, Jr. "United States Involvement in Standardization of Testing Methods." Address before the International Standards Organization, September 13, 1972.

American Petroleum Institute. "Publications and Materials." 1972.

——. Wallace Seward, letter dated July 28, 1972.

American Society of Civil Engineers. William French, letter dated April 9, 1970.

——. Interviews with members, past national and local officers, Professor Biggs, M.I.T.; M. N. Clair, Thompson and Lichtner; Professor Spencer, Northeastern, Spring 1970.

American Society of Mechanical Engineers. "Council Policy: Guide to Society Legislative Activities."

——. William E. Reaser, letter dated March 6, 1970.

——. Interviews with members, past national and local officers, H. W. Emmons, Harvard; H. H. Hemenway, Western Precipitation; Earle C. Miller, Riley Stoker; Spring 1970.

American Society for Testing and Materials. "ASTM and the Voluntary Standardization System," 1969.

——. Book of ASTM Standards.

——. F. J. Mardulier, "ASTM: Its Function and Philosophy."

——. F. J. Mardulier, "Is There a Future for Voluntary Standardization?" Address at ASTM Winter Meeting, January 31, 1967.

Association of Home Appliance Manufacturers. Herbert Phillips, letter dated July 28, 1972.

Color Association of the United States. Midge Wilson, letter dated July 14, 1972.

Comics Magazine Association of America. Code of the CMAA, 1972.

——. Leonard Darvin, letter dated July 6, 1972.

Consumers Union. Morris Kaplan, letter dated March 5, 1970.

Engineers Joint Council. "Directory of Engineering Societies," 1970.

——. Symposium. G. W. McCullough, "Relationship between Engineering Societies and Industry." Speech given January 18, 1965.

Institute of Electrical and Electronics Engineers. H. L. Nichol, letter dated April 17, 1970.

——. Interview with former national officer Professor Mimno, Harvard, Spring 1970.

Manufacturers Standardization Society of the Valve and Fittings Industry, letter dated August 9, 1972.

National Association of Purchasing Agents. "Standardization Manual: A Book of Principles and Practices for Purchasing Agents," 1964.

National Fire Protection Association. "NFPA," 1972.

Paper Stationery and Tablet Manufacturers Association. Standards Research Committee. "Recommended Standards and Specifications for Tablets and Related Products," 1964.

Shoe Lace Manufacturers Association (defunct). "A Manual of Standards," 1966. (See Norther Textile Association.)

Society of Automotive Engineers. "SAE in Profile."

——. Interview with SAE member, Professor Rogowski, M.I.T., Spring 1970.

Underwriters Laboratories. "Testing for Public Safety."

Index

About the Author

Science-Technology-Society Interactions

David Hemenway received his A.B. from Harvard in 1966, and an M.A. in economics from the University of Michigan the next year. After briefly working as an executive trainee in the Pentagon, he became Washington Correspondent for Consumers Union. He returned to Harvard to receive his Ph.D. in 1974. He has been an instructor at Harvard and Wellesley and Assistant Professor at Boston University. Presently (January 1975) he is economic assistant to Judge Edelstein who is trying the Justice Department's antitrust suit against I.B.M. His previous published works have been in association with Ralph Nader task groups concerning government regulation of business.